ONCE UPON
A RHYME

IMAGINATION FOR
A NEW GENERATION

Dorset
Edited by Kelly Oliver

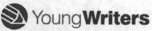 Young**Writers**

First published in Great Britain in 2004 by:
Young Writers
Remus House
Coltsfoot Drive
Peterborough
PE2 9JX
Telephone: 01733 890066
Website: www.youngwriters.co.uk

SB ISBN 1 84460 445 4

Foreword

Young Writers was established in 1991 and has been passionately devoted to the promotion of reading and writing in children and young adults ever since. The quest continues today. Young Writers remains as committed to engendering the fostering of burgeoning poetic and literary talent as ever.

This year's Young Writers competition has proven as vibrant and dynamic as ever and we are delighted to present a showcase of the best poetry from across the UK. Each poem has been carefully selected from a wealth of *Once Upon A Rhyme* entries before ultimately being published in this, our twelfth primary school poetry series.

Once again, we have been supremely impressed by the overall high quality of the entries we have received. The imagination, energy and creativity which has gone into each young writer's entry made choosing the best poems a challenging and often difficult but ultimately hugely rewarding task - the general high standard of the work submitted amply vindicating this opportunity to bring their poetry to a larger appreciative audience.

We sincerely hope you are pleased with our final selection and that you will enjoy *Once Upon A Rhyme Dorset* for many years to come.

Contents

Park School

Lauren Goodwin (8)	53
Giselle Yonace (8)	54
Timothy Radvan (9)	54
Lydia Ainsworth (8)	55
Henry Turner (11)	55
Abigail Coward (9)	56
James Sidwick (8)	56
Eloise Dudley (9)	56
Ava Hawkins (9)	57
Karl Al-Omar (8)	57
Daniel Couto-Poci (9)	57
Sophie Watton (10)	58
Dominic Lees-Bell (8)	58
Ryan Crooks (10)	59
Ryan Frankel (8)	59

Portesham Primary School

Chloe Keefe Barton (9)	60
Louise Morris (9)	60
Chloe Snuggs (10)	60
Daniel Burnett (10)	60
Adam Snape (10)	61
Jack Taylor (11)	61
Sian Hennessy (10)	61
Rachel Mayo (10)	61
Livia Peterkin (9)	62
Charlotte Barlow (10)	62
Chloe Mackenzie (7)	63
Ellena Minns (9)	63
Anna Freiesleben (9)	64
Lee Thomas Williamson (9)	64
Maisie Dean (7)	65
Molly Booker (7)	65
Meredith Harman (9)	66
Katie Wilson (9)	67
Amy Taylor (8)	68
Lisa Robinson (9)	68
Daniel Jones (11)	68
Abigail Booker (8)	69
Matthew Alvis (9)	69

Robert Harrington (10)	69
Jack Bellworthy (7)	70
Laura Croxson (10)	70
Scarlet Moon (11)	70

Port Regis School

Charlotte Sutton (9)	71
Edward Macdonald (8)	71
Zeta Leung (9)	72
Patrick Milne (9)	72
Flora McFarlane (9)	73
Jack Gething (8)	73
Anna Gray (8)	74
Elizabeth Killick (8)	75
Scarlett Aichroth (8)	75
Sophie Cahill (8)	76
Emily Matthews (9)	76
George Butler (10)	77
Freddy Bunbury (11)	77
Jazz Bisset (10)	78
Jamie Horton (8)	78
Lizzie Potts (11)	79
Gabriel Dorey (9)	79
Eliza Hamer (10)	80
Eloise Smail (11)	80
Toby Mather (10)	81
Amy Watson (10)	81
Wil Milligan (10)	82
Jack Deverell (8)	82
Madeleine Vaughan (10)	83
Lloyd Wallace (8)	83
Chris Pudner (11)	84
Alex Sage (10)	84
Philippa Kerby (10)	85
Timothy Dickens (8)	86
Kathryn Francis (8)	86
Anders Horwood (8)	86
Joseph Tuersley (8)	87
Benedict Judd (8)	87
James Pullen (8)	87
Chloe Jacout (9)	88

Marcus Willis (11)	88
Natasha Collins (10)	89
Alistair John Hughes (11)	89
Cameron Mackie (9)	90
Bridget Harris (11)	90
Christopher Brinkworth (10)	91
Harriet Hedges (9)	91
Lucy Lloyd-Williams (11)	92
Daisy Kerby (7)	92
Saskia Tempest-Radford (10)	93
Lara Good (9)	93
Samantha Pearce (11)	94
Jack Ruddy (9)	94
Patrick Allen (11)	94
Max Austin-Little (10)	95
Nick Meares (11)	95

St Mary's CE Primary School, Bridport

Hazel Goldman (10)	95
Billie Goldman (10)	96
Lauren Ford (9)	96
Amica Dickson (9)	97
Louise Bottle (10)	97

St Michael's CE VA Primary School, Lyme Regis

Leif Sanders (10)	98
Samantha Bird (9)	98
Antonia Gamage (9)	99
Eleanor Shoesmith (10)	99
Robyn Lewis (9)	100
Lillie Filtness (10)	101
Keiren White (10)	102
Charlie Taylor (9)	103
Tom Wood (9)	104
Billie-Mae Hoole (10)	105
Poppy Kitcher (9)	106
Amy Hanlon (9)	106
Ryan Wood (9)	107
Rebecca Solway (9)	107
Phoebe Moksher Hill (9)	108
Katie Austin (10)	109

Salway Ash CE Primary School
Alex Hoskins (10)   127
Finn Buchanan-Brown (10)   128
Gabby Duff (10)   129

Thornford CE (VA) Primary School
Katie Bakewell (10)   129
Rob Helyar (11)   130
Peter Miller (10)   130
Chloe Beard (11)   131
Sam Jones (10)   131
Lauren Peters (10)   132
Jamie Appleby (9)   132
Megan Taylor (11)   133
Ellie Horsfield (10)   133
Jonathon Legg (9)   134
Isobel Carretta (9)   135
Rachel Akerman (10)   136
Tezra Sculthorpe (9)   136
Vivienne Greening (10)   137
Aaron FitzGerald (10)   137
Paul Manton (10)   138
Charlotte Mouncey (9)   138
Hayley Peters (10)   139
Nathan Thompson (9)   139
Jonathan Dolbear (10)   140
Will Davies (9)   141
Charlotte Gordge (10)   142
Alex Thorne (9)   142

The Poems

Rapunzel

Once upon a time
In a kingdom long ago
Lived a princess all alone
Who slept in a tower
Watching out down below
For a prince to come calling
Saying more than just 'Hello.'
To save her from her loneliness
She needed him by her side.

'Hark do I hear him
Calling out my precious love.'
'Rapunzel, Rapunzel, let down your hair.'
'OK, be with you in a minute.'
The prince started to climb.
Snap!
'Oh drat, I must remember to get some stronger hair extensions
That's the fifth pair this week!'

Sophie Atkinson (10)
All Saints Primary School

A Dragon And His Jokes

Deep in his lair the dragon sits,
Roaming the books for bits
And bobs about jokes.
Going to get his coat,
Now setting up a mechanical goat,
Screaming for help, because he's fallen in the moat.

Charlie Knight (10)
All Saints Primary School

Baldylox And The Bears

Baldylox awoke one morning,
What a great day for a walk, he thought.
So he left his porridge to cool
And set off into the forest.
Just then a family of bears walked by.
'Ah ha,' they said, 'what a lovely smell.'
They barged in and all sat round
To eat a lovely bowl of porridge.
'Yummy,' they said and smacked their lips.
They leant back in their chairs.
Suddenly they found themselves on the floor.
The little one cried, 'My tummy hurts.'
So they trailed upstairs to Baldylox's bedroom.
'Phew, somewhere we can lie down,' they sighed.
Just then Baldylox returned.
What a sight to see; his front door
Hanging on its hinges, his chairs in splinters.
There was no sight of his porridge.
Baldylox barged upstairs and shouted,
'Get out of my house.'
He grabbed each bear by its collar,
And threw them outside.

Robert Salt (10)
All Saints Primary School

Chickens In The Snow

Watching from my window,
A white blanket covering the ground,
I see my chicken house standing in the snow,
The cockerel sound is a sign to them,
That feeding time's beginning,
Barging as they follow him out,
High stepping through the snow.

Deanya Bailey (11)
All Saints Primary School

Old Farmer Smithers

Old Farmer Smithers was on his spreader
The dung flying over the field
He hit a cow and knocked it down
Then revved and spun around.

Old Farmer Smithers was on his tractor
The cow tied firmly to his axle
Smithers pulled with a heave and a ho
But the cow stayed down in the hollow
So he revved and spun around.

Old Farmer Smithers was on his quad
Trying hard to rescue his cow
Along came his wife, all trouble and strife
So the cow jumped up and ran around.

Ashley White (11)
All Saints Primary School

Cinderella

C inders sits alone by the fire
I nstead of laughing, she cries
'N obody loves me,' she sobs in
D espair. Suddenly, in a flash of
E normous sparks, a fairy did appear.
'R eally!' exclaimed the fairy to her.
'E legance is what you'll be
L ike a princess of the stars we'll see'
L aughing, waving, as she appeared, but her
A nxious sisters waited in fear.

Charlotte Armstrong (10)
All Saints Primary School

Cinderella

Cinders sits sadly by the dancing flames,
Her clothes are in tatters, her sisters call her names.
Her life is dreadful, hard and unfair,
Till one night her fairy godmother stands right there.

'You shall go to the ball,' she announces,
'Go fetch these things before the cat pounces.'
Suddenly Cinderella looks lovely and bright.
'Off to the ball, but don't dance all night.'

The palace shines bright, very glamorous with gold.
People dance and chatter, it's a sight to behold.
The prince spies Cinderella and falls madly in love,
But the two ugly sisters give her a great big shove.

Poor Cinderella sits all alone,
There's a knock at the door, but they say she's not at home.
The prince stands before her, her shoe in his hand.
It fits! She's a princess, the happiest in the land.

Jodi-Ann Hall (10)
All Saints Primary School

Snow White

S now White, lovely and sweet,
N o one wished to harm her as
O n the bed of glass she slept.
W hile the dwarfs stood quietly

W aiting, wondering, when the
H andsome prince would suddenly appear.
I n a flash he had dismounted.
T enderly kissed her rosy-red lips
E agerly, to live happily ever after.

Tara Myles (11)
All Saints Primary School

Sleeping Beauty's Boyfriends

In a high tower,
Above a green mossy lake,
There was a girl,
Who slept waiting for a prince.
One day Prince Charming arrived at the castle,
He kissed Sleeping Beauty's rosy-red lips,
She didn't stir,

Her pink flowing dress waved in the wind,
Her eyes fluttered open,
Like a rose opening its petals,
She opened her eyes,
And saw Prince Charming,
She then said, 'You can go now,'
She pulled a list out from underneath her bed,
And ticked Prince Charming's name,
Prince Charming was taken aback,
She thought for a moment,
'I'll give you a grade 3 out of 10,
It was an OK kiss but I've had better.'
She swung her legs over the bed and fell back to sleep.

The next day she heard someone shouting from outside,
It was Prince Philip!
He was calling, 'Rapunzel, Rapunzel!'
Sleeping Beauty shouted back, 'Rapunzel doesn't live here,
                         she lives at number 20, Tower View,
Anyway what do you want with her?
She's busy with her hair extensions,
And I've got to get ready for my coffee morning with her,
Last time you were here, you got a grade 1 on kissing.'
Sleeping Beauty had her coffee morning with Rapunzel,
The she went to bed waiting for the next prince to come along,
Which won't be long, she thought to herself.

Penny-Anne Yeulet (10)
All Saints Primary School

Fire

The fire crackles, like popcorn in a microwave.
Tiny sparks fly into the air like fireworks.
Flames begin to dance like ballerinas,
Flickering and casting shadows all around like a haunted house.

First the flames are an over ripe orange,
Then they turn yellow,
With small tinges of blue.
The heat is really powerful,
It burns and my face tingles as I stand watching it gleam.

The fire crackles again like popcorn in a microwave,
It sounds as if a hundred witches are crackling their potions.
As evening draws on,
The flames die down like shooting stars,
The embers remain,
Glowing brightly like the sun dying down.

Beverley Green (9)
Chickerell Primary School

I Once Met A Princess

I once met a princess
And she was very nice
And she was very beautiful
She was made of sugar and spice

I once met a princess
She invited me to tea
We played all day, we played all night
I am glad that she asked me

I once met a princess
She was my best friend for that day
I hope I see her again some day.

Ria Banwell (7)
Chickerell Primary School

My Sunflower

My sunflower has died,
The tallest flower in the garden,
Not a dull flower,
But a bright yellow flower.

Standing in the garden,
Making it look bright,
The leaves waving.

No more light gardens,
No more lovely leaves,
No more happiness in the garden,
No more tall hairy stalks.

My sunflower has died,
Its swaying big leaves,
Not a dull flower,
But a bright yellow flower.

Carly Baber (10)
Chickerell Primary School

Harvest Fayre

All the fruits and vegetables
Are packed neatly into a box
Ready to be shipped away
So as not to be eaten by a fox.

The children with kind hearts
Put the boxes in a car
They take them to the village
And travel very far.

They knock at the doors
Of the people who are lonely
And give them the harvest
Which is oh, so lovely!

Jay Farley (8)
Chickerell Primary School

A Winter Day

It's a winter day,
a winter day
we love to
go outside
and play

It's cold and crisp,
soft and fluffy
the time of
year to
wear a muffy

Slipping and sleighing
and sliding we go
we've had so much
fun in the snow

The amount of fun
we've had in the snow
our faces are
all aglow

Shortly it will
be time to go
we've had our
fun in the snow.

Emma Mumford (8)
Chickerell Primary School

The Dreamcatcher

The dreamcatcher's middle is like a spider's web
Its colour is as blue as a clear ocean
Silky feathers dangle from the catcher,
Like leaves on a big tree.

I puzzle over the holes in the middle
It seems the nightmares are escaping
That must not be true
I wonder why there are holes in the middle?

And then the feathers make me think
Of the new duckling born in spring
A new life begins, flowers open after a long sleep
Think how nice that is.

As I lie in my bed I can picture an evil dream,
Water witches in a rough sea
I hear a swoosh which is the feathers of the protector
Stopping my bad imagination.

The maker made this dreamcatcher
With an upsetting memory
He made it to stop him
Being woken in the night

Saying,
　　'I am a man with an unlucky past
　　I made this with no feelings at all
　　But hope for a happier future to come.'

Bethan Hutton (9)
Chickerell Primary School

African Safari

I'm snuggled by the fire
as it is cold and chilly outside
I wish I were somewhere hot . . .

I wish I were on an African safari
I imagine drumming and the blazing hot sun.

I wish I could spy a herd of elephants
so gentle with their graceful trunks.

I wish I could see giraffes
standing tall with their elegant necks.

I wish I could see a pride of lions
playing with their baby cubs.

I wish I could spot a cheetah
racing past like a Porsche 911.

I wish I could see these amazing,
awesome animals,
perhaps one day I will!

Camilla Llewellyn (8)
Chickerell Primary School

My Cat

My cat is so pretty
She is fluffy and cute
Her colour is tabby
And she is always so happy
She sometimes is naughty
But mostly is kind
I love my cat Bagpuss
Because she is mine.

Tyler Flood (8)
Chickerell Primary School

Living Flames, Dying Embers

Fire crackling in the midnight sky
Dancing flames stretching so high
Fingers of orange, fingers of red
Swirling like fish on the seabed

Burning our eyes with this dazzling sight
Flames that can warm us in the dead of the night
Warming our hands by the embers of heat,
Waving as if our eyes to greet

An angry cat reaching out, just like a spitting dragon
It grows and grows till all is gone
Fire fighting battles,
Sounds just like witches' cackles

Like heat from the sun is this great mass of fire
It's not going any higher
Slowly, slowly as the flames die away
Smoke and darkness have nothing to say.

Lorna Campbell (10)
Chickerell Primary School

The One-Legged Freak

The one-legged freak had a job to speak
Because he didn't have any teeth,
One eye was blue, one eye was green
The funniest freak I've ever seen

His clothes were rickety, tattered and torn,
Not the type you'd wear in a storm,
His toe was poking out of his shoe,
Oh dear, what a to-do!

Jack Jolliffe (8)
Chickerell Primary School

My Friend Flicka

He is tall, chestnut and cheeky, with a flowing mane and tail
His snowy white socks and blaze, glisten in the sunlight
He is kind, gentle and fun-loving and always ready to play
Together we ride round the countryside taking in the beautiful sights
      He is my friend Flicka

I am so lucky to have a pony of my own, the work I do not mind
Feeding, cleaning, grooming each and every day
He shows me that he is grateful for all that I do
He is a great big softie whose best friend's called Pooh
      He is my friend Flicka

He gallops around the field, bucking and tossing his head
I can hear the thud of his hooves pounding on the ground
He's like a wild horse, running with his herd
He loves to play so much, he has a taste of freedom
      He is my friend Flicka

He grazes quietly on the lush green grass
And can eat a carrot whole
Food is just his favourite thing
How quickly his bowl becomes empty
      He is my friend Flicka

My pony is not just any pony, he has a very posh name,
He is registered 'Peasdown Rembrandt'
His style shows as he jumps and trots
Such very strong, elegant paces
      He is my friend Flicka

How very, very lucky I am
To have such a special friend
Someone to share the special times
Today, tomorrow and always
      He is my *best* friend Flicka!

Reah Bailey (9)
Chickerell Primary School

Sweet Autumn

The cold wind feels like frosty snow
So now I know it's cold.
Berries glisten in the golden sun
But it won't be long before they're old.

The slippery grass feels
Like a wet slimy snake.
The mud on the ground begins to clump
It looks like it needs a rake.

The fat chubby slug looks
Like a charging angry bull.
There's a yield in the field,
The flowers and corn are very tall.

The glistening berries shine
In the golden sunlight.
The children jump in the crispy leaves
And the leaves fly through the sky light.

Briony Bonnett (8)
Chickerell Primary School

My Pet Dog

Cat-chaser
Door-barker
Mud-scratcher
Chair-licker
People-sniffer
Food-muncher
Sinead-licker
Biscuit-barker
End of Mum's bed-sleeper

Sinead Smith (10)
Christ the King RC Primary School

Kennings School

Ball-kicker,
Pencil-flicker,

Sports day-racer,
Ball-chaser,

Rubbish-binner,
Sports day-winner,

Maths-teacher,
Science-cheater,

Detention-taker,
Illness-faker,

Science-whizzer,
Liquid-fizzer,

Book-reader,
Bird-feeder.

Joseph Elliott (11)
Christ the King RC Primary School

Kennings Gerbils

Cardboard-eater
Ball-runner
Fur-scratcher
Good-hider
Water-sucker
Food-flinger
Tail-flinger
Sawdust-digger.

Michael Ellerby (10)
Christ the King RC Primary School

The Ocean

The ocean can be ferocious,
The ocean can be strong.
I watch the seagulls soar by,
As they sing their happy song!

The ocean can be smelly,
The ocean can be sweet.
As I walk along the silky sand,
It massages my feet!

The ocean can be green,
The ocean can be blue.
As I swim along in my rubber ring,
I know the sea is true.

I am leaving the ocean now,
I have had a really fun time.
I know it's very disappointing,
But this poem has ended its rhyme.

Joanna Treggiden (9)
Christ the King RC Primary School

Christina Aguilera

Hi Christina, my name is Dan,
I love your music, I'm your biggest fan,
Your ever-changing hair and clothes you wear,
Makes everybody stop and stare,
My favourite song is 'Can't Hold Us Down'
And when I hear Britney, it makes me frown!
Your catchy songs and powerful voice,
Make you, Christina, my first choice!

Danniella Reilly (11)
Christ the King RC Primary School

Kennings Lord Of The Rings

(In the fire of Adam's mind, one ring to rule them all)

Axe-basher
People-scarer
Dark-rider
Ring-bearer
Sword-slasher
Troll-maker
Orc-slayer
Blood-splatterer.

Adam Johnstone (10)
Christ the King RC Primary School

Kennings Falcon

Beak-snapper
Wing-flapper

Fast-flyer
Night-cryer

Mouse-eater
Water-drinker

Rabbit-catcher
Claw-scratcher

Wing-glider
Water-strider.

Matthew Butler (11)
Christ the King RC Primary School

Kennings Teacher

Star-giver
Coffee-drinker
Whistle-blower
House team point-giver
Literacy-teacher
Golden rule-setter
That's Mrs Lord, the best *teacher!*

Courtney Dodge (10)
Christ the King RC Primary School

The Spirit Of Rockwell Sea

Is he here? Is he there? Can you see him anywhere?
In the silence of the night can you feel him without a fright?
Can you feel him? Can you see him? Is he there?
Can you hear his voice taunting the night to come alive.
I hear voices muttering like a ghost.
I hear screaming like sailors' stubble.
I see ships in the shadows sinking to their death,
no more breath . . .

Samantha Coombs (10)
Christ the King RC Primary School

My Parents Are Aliens

My parents are *aliens*
They've got fuzzy hair
Everything I do, they have to stand and stare
I can't tell *anyone* but they've got their own lair
But my parents are aliens
And it's just not fair!

Leigh-Anne Dady (10)
Christ the King RC Primary School

Sweets

S   is for sweet taste, it's a shame to waste.
W   is for Wonka bars, the pop will send you to Mars.
E   is for Egg Harrie bows, they'll make your tongue glow.
E   is for eclairs, they're so sweet, they'll attract bears.
T   is for toffee, it's so sweet, it will make you thirsty for coffee.
S   is for scrumptious and that is exactly what you'll get.

Chloe de Silva (10)
Christ the King RC Primary School

Kennings Lord Of The Rings

(This poem was made in the fire of Sarah Crease's mind)

Power-ruler
Sword-dweller

Adventure-hunter
Spear-blinker

Orc-stayer
Horn-player

Bow-caster
Magic-master

Nazgul-Flyer
Little-liar

Ring-carrier
Black-barrier

Web-spinner
Hobbit-dinner

High-blinker
Slow-thinker

Eager-fighter
Finger-biter.

Sarah Joy Crease (10)
Christ the King RC Primary School

The Writer Of This Poem

(Based on 'The Writer Of This Poem' by Roger McGough)

Is as quick as a cheetah
As naughty as you could imagine
As good as David Beckham at football
And definitely is a skater.

Dale Adamson (9)
Christ the King RC Primary School

The Dragon's Eye

The dragon's eye,
Sparkles in the sun.
He is an only dragon,
He is the only one.

The dragon's eye,
Is small and beady.
He flies really quick,
He is really speedy.

The dragon's eye,
Is as fast as its owner.
He is really slick,
Just like a loner.

The dragon's eye,
Has a lair of his own.
He eats in it,
Hmmm! Maybe a nice bone!

The dragon's eye,
Would like to go on a hunt.
He would quite like a rabbit,
Or maybe a piglet runt!

The dragon's eye,
Likes to sleep alone.
Not with his other eye,
Just alone, all alone, in his quiet, peaceful home.

Hannah Martin (9)
Christ the King RC Primary School

Spaghetti

Spaghetti, spaghetti,
I'll gobble you up.
Spaghetti, spaghetti,
I can't get enough.
Spaghetti, spaghetti,
You're slimy and strong.
Spaghetti, spaghetti,
Just come along.
Spaghetti, spaghetti,
I'll gobble you up.
Spaghetti, spaghetti,
I can't get enough.
Spaghetti, spaghetti,
You're slimy and strong.
Spaghetti, spaghetti,
Just come along.

Amy O'Friel (10)
Christ the King RC Primary School

I Like This Poem

I like this poem
It came this morning
It is as big as a buffalo
It is as loud as a crowd

I like this poem
It came this morning
It is as cool as cucumber
It is as wild as the wind

I like this poem
It came this morning
It came this morning
Cool, it's amazing!

Kelly Dady (10)
Christ the King RC Primary School

My Dream

My dream is to swim with dolphins so wild and free,
To feel my hair blowing like glinting waves so wild, so free.
My dream is to hear the rippling waters beyond my very feet,
To feel my toes being washed with the cool ripples
Of the glistening blue sheet.

My dream is to dance over rushing waters of the glinting sea.
Make it happen, please, please.
My dream is to swim with dolphins, I dream of it every night,
When I'm snug and tight in my bed, I dream of them every night.

Chiara Grace Gattuso (10)
Christ the King RC Primary School

Word Of A Lie

I am the best singer and dancer in my family
and that's no word of a lie.
I love music
and that's no word of a lie.
My best friends are Abbie and Rhianne
and that's no word of a lie.
My best singer is Avril Lavigne
and that's no word of a lie.
I was born in Bournemouth hospital
and that's no word of a lie.
I live in Kinson in Bournemouth
and that's no word of a lie.

Siobhan Breakingbury (8)
Christ the King RC Primary School

Ocean

Ocean's sleek calm face
It's silk and runs at a slow pace!
It streams in the night,
And yes, it is so very bright!

It's kind of green
And oh so seen!
Oh what is in it?
The seaweed on the sea sits!

Ocean is a restful place
Oh how, oh how it warms my face!

Megan Sian Barrington (9)
Christ the King RC Primary School

The Writer Of This Poem

(Based on 'The Writer Of This Poem' by Roger McGough)

The writer of this poem is as big as a giant,
As cold as ice,
As cunning as a fox,
As tall as a giraffe.
And that is the end of my rhyme.

Sophie Gallagher (10)
Christ the King RC Primary School

The Blue Fairy

Flutter, flutter, go their wings.
Their soft voices as they sing.
Gently floating through the air.
My lovely blue fairy disappears
In the air.

Sophie Squibb (10)
Christ the King RC Primary School

Hi Snail!

Slithery snail slides silently across gritty, bumpy ground.
With his spiral shell he slides along
Leaving a silver tinfoil trail behind him.
Slow snail goes as slow as a punctured tyre on a car,
With his stalk-eyed eyes and his spiral shell.
He slithers silently into gardens.
He's a gardener's worst enemy!
He nibbles all night, he nibbles all day!

Jaz Roper (7)
Greenford CE Primary School

Armoured Snail

Slow snail with hard swirling shell of buttercup-yellow armour.
Protection from birds.
Newly-planted plants.
Gardeners' terrorist!
Slimy snail slithers silently leaving sparkling trails of slime,
Shining like dew in the morning sun.

Darwin Culley (8)
Greenford CE Primary School

Stalk-Eyed Beasts

Slow, slimy, stalk-eyed snail
Slides through rattling grass.
Ferocious snail leaves golden slime on garden bricks.
Bright sun shines on the snail's beautiful yellow shell.

Sam Bridle (8)
Greenford CE Primary School

Seal Cry

I watch my friends flit by,
Each day less of them,
We swim and then we die,
We glide gracefully, gently along,
The harpoon strikes!
It takes a life,
It kills, like the knife,
It is endangering us,
Endangering our friends,
We must be careful,
Humans just play with their trends,
And kill us, out of existence,
The black tangle of death,
Floats through the deep blue ocean,
My friends,
Wave-makers,
The dolphins and whales,
Caught!
They disappear,
Soon, we'll all disappear,
Man will have nothing to eat,
Their turn to witness pain . . .
Instead of us . . . !

Andrew Hobbs (10)
Greenford CE Primary School

Slimy Snail

Warning gardeners!
Slimy snail will attack your garden.
It eats down garden plants.
It moves silently to your vegetables,
Leaving a see-through, silver trail.
It is brown with gold, silver and green stripes.

Harry Johnson (8)
Greenford CE Primary School

Whispers Of The Whales

I see it . . .
Its sleek bold body, shaped in sand.
Its cursing deep grey eyes
getting revenge on the sparkling, calm, blue sea.
Now it listens to the waves
thinking,
What went wrong?
How did I end up here?
With a few last strong breaths like an engine being turned off,
Big Blue lies there.
The sun blazes on his dry flesh.
Whispers of his pleading, sound no longer.
His friends are calling to him,
but no longer can he hear.
So then, no longer will pain
cast through the ocean.
His drumming heart comes to an end.

Claire Anne Hobbs (10)
Greenford CE Primary School

Snails

Slithering slimy buttercup snails,
gently slide silently,
leaving sticky trails,
of silver tinfoil.

Armoured snails slither
along the moist soil,
which leads to
juicy, tender,
green vegetables,
that snails munch up.
Full up!

Anika Gardner (8)
Greenford CE Primary School

Whales' Lives

The shimmering water of the ocean
Glides round the whale,
As it easily sails through the water like a boat.
Imagine if it was you!
What would it be like?

Whales crying for life,
Pleading to be free,
Trapped in a massive mesh net
Unable to see a thing,
Imagine if it was you!
What would it be like?

Whales in tanks, demanding to be free.
Some live,
Some die in that horrible place.
Imagine if it was you!
What would it be like?

Whales were the citizens of the sea.
As they sing their lonely song
Their friends drop slowly down to the ocean floor.

Imagine every sea creature in the world, gone!
What would that be like?

Tragic!

Aleisa Whitcombe (11)
Greenford CE Primary School

Gruesome Snails

They munch up plants like a vacuum cleaner,
At dawn you spot the green and silver trails,
Eating cabbage, carrots, broccoli and fruit,
Gardeners and snails are worst enemies,
Slimy snails slither through rotten garden leaves,
Snails, the gardeners' terror!

Gareth Provis (7)
Greenford CE Primary School

Slimy Snail

Slithery snail glides down the rocky, hard path
leaving a slimy trail behind.
Gardeners' worst enemy - vegetable-eating monster.
Silent slow snail carries a protective shell
on his back, spiral-shelled home, buttercup colour.
When danger approaches, he curls up in his armoured shell.

Molly Neville (8)
Greenford CE Primary School

The Dog Down The Road

A vicious little monster,
Living down the road.
With a snarl like a gangster,
And a very heavy load.

He has razor-sharp teeth,
And a very hard stare.
He will make you into a child feast,
With you as the top layer.

He will sit down and scream all night,
Until he hears his call.
I always think he wants a fight,
When the day is about to fall.

But now I think I've grown up,
And tall enough to see,
He's only just a little pup,
And he won't like me for tea.

Although he has a bit of a sharp tooth,
And likes to pull a face,
Now I know he's not hard, uncouth,
He only wanted to chew my lace.

Natasha Lianne Carter (8)
Hillbourne Middle School

The Four Seasons Of The Year!

Spring is the first season of the year,
With all the births it's a season of cheer,
Daffodils often grow in spring,
The soft humming of birds sounds like a sweet bell ring,
With all the flowers in the windows,
Out in the country the river softly flows,
And summer shortly draws nearer and nearer!

Summer is the time when you all go out,
When there are not many daffodils about,
You're all at the beach topping up your tan,
And what makes it even hotter, is your lunch in the pan,
The children go in the sea for a dip,
And wake up all the fish from their summer kip,
Often boats whizz on by,
While up in the sky the seagulls fly,
And autumn shortly draws nearer and nearer!

There's a wonderful feeling that buzzes up inside,
And all I want to do is spread my joy wide,
I love autumn, so, so much,
I don't like it out of my grubby hands' clutch,
The brown and the green and the beautiful gold,
To me autumn never gets old,
And winter shortly draws nearer and nearer!

I love wonderful winter,
When all the icicles start to glitter,
And even if it's bitterly cold,
The sun comes out and is big and bold,
What takes place are parties and celebrations,
It goes on and on throughout all the nations,
But now it goes back to the start of spring!

Eleanor Pickford (8)
Hillbourne Middle School

Keeley

Keeley is my sister
She screams and shouts all day
But the best bit is
I love her just the same

She drinks like a fish
And sleeps like a dog
But the best bit is
I love her just the same

She giggles and plays all the days
And tries to sit up, always gives up
But the best bit is
I love her just the same

She is five months old
And her hands are always cold
But the best bit is
I love her just the same

You can't get enough of her
My auntie's always round
But the best bit is
I love her just the same

She likes watching Tweenies
And plays with my Beanies
But the best bit is
I love her just the same

She scratches my face and pulls my hair
So when I am near I have to take care
But the best bit is
I love her just the same.

Shannon Harris (8)
Hillbourne Middle School

Feelings

Peace is white,
It smells like fruit on a tree.
Peace tastes like butter on peas,
It sounds like birds singing,
It feels smooth.
Peace lives in your heart.

War is black,
It smells like a rotting, disgusting stench,
War tastes like burnt leftovers,
It sounds like the Devil laughing,
It feels bumpy and rough.
War lives in Hell.

Happiness is pink,
It smells like flowers,
Happiness tastes like sweets,
It sounds like children playing,
It feels soft.
Happiness lives in the air.

Jealousy is green,
It smells like mouldy cheese,
Jealousy tastes like sour milk,
It sounds like a wailing cat,
It feels hot and sticky.
Jealousy lives in the shadows.

Anthony Dale (9)
Hillbourne Middle School

Our Cat's Bad Day

Our cat's bad day is just on its way,
A door slammed shut on her tail,
I've never heard such a loud wail,
The situation is far from funny,
Don't let's worry about the money,
If the vet says she'll die,
I'll make sure I say goodbye,
But I want her to stay alive,
For a fit, healthy cat, we will strive,
Now her stitched tail is bandaged and red,
A cone like a lampshade surrounds her head.
I thank God she's back home,
With her bandage and cone,
Now she's asleep on her bed.
I want to play but I'll let her rest instead.

Joseph Benham (9)
Hillbourne Middle School

The Twelve Months Of The Year

January is the first month of the year
February, you send a valentine to someone dear
March sees spring lambs bouncing about
April showers is when umbrellas come out
May, we visit parks and have loads of fun
June's halfway through the year with lots of sun
July, school finishes and children are free
August has holidays on the beach by the sea
September starts a new year of school
October's got Hallowe'en when witches rule
November sees fireworks sparkling and bright
December's when Christmas trees twinkle with lights.

Nicola Jayne Button (9)
Hillbourne Middle School

The Dentist Appointment

On the 7th of July
We went to the dentist's
Then we went into the waiting room
The receptionist called our name.

Chorus   *People by people*
Into the surgery
All to see the dentist
With a tooth emergency.

I went into the room
For my filling
I had two injections
And they were killin'.

People by people
Into the surgery
All to see the dentist
With a tooth emergency.

He used the drill
I started to shake
When it was done
My mum bought me a cake.

People by people
Into the surgery
All to see the dentist
With a tooth emergency.

Rhi-anne Budden (10)
Hillbourne Middle School

Time To Stop Pollution

Imagine the ocean with all life gone,
Without the breaching whales
Or a beluga's song.

Without sea horses to gently glide,
Or jellyfish to float,
Or a friendly dolphin pod, that dares to chase your boat.

No clownfish, no angelfish, or a beautiful coral reef,
No hammerhead,
Or great white shark with rows of scary teeth.

No octopus's tentacles to slither on the ground
No starfishes to lie there,
Without a single sound.

No sea horses, no turtles or a spiky anemone,
Or the many other creatures
That live beneath the sea.

To stop this becoming the dreadful truth
I know a simple solution
Take Nature's hand and make a stand,
It's time to stop pollution!

Sophie Allisett (9)
Hillbourne Middle School

Playtime

Playtime's for kids, playtime means fun
Some getting hurt but some still have fun.
Teachers are watching, silent and alert
And catching the bullies that throw the dirt.
The small kids are snoozing bored of work.
The girls and boys are playing 'Stuck'
And the rest of the boys are jumping in mud.
Then the bell rings, there is a silence
The class cards are lifted, the children rush in.

Matthew Sawyer (9)
Hillbourne Middle School

Going To The Beach

One summer's day, heading down to the coast.
Up at dawn before the sun rises high in the sky
I have to pack my beach towel, trunks and my bucket and spade.
We pass fields carpeted in green with black and white flecks.
I wonder whether the cows are ready for milking yet.
As I arrive I can see miles of golden sand.
People building sandcastles.
Granny is knitting in her deckchair
Grandpa is smoking his pipe
And the sea is swishing gently against the rocks
But what I like best is ice-cold lemonade with a dash of lime
And an ice cream melting in the midday sun, dripping slowly
                                              upon my knee.

Jake Burton (10)
Hillbourne Middle School

Questions?

Why is the sky blue?
Why do I like you?
How high up is up?
Why do I drink from a cup?
Who invented money?
Why do bees make honey?
How old is God?
Where is the Land of Nod?
How long is a piece of string?
Why does a bell go *ding*?
Why is water clear?
Why am I here?

Chelsea Brown (11)
Hillbourne Middle School

Good Girls And Bad Boys!

Girls are good, and boys are bad.
Girls have beauty, and boys are mad.
Girls are sad when boys are bad.
Boys are glad that they are mad.
Girls have colour, and boys are dull.
Girls clean up, because boys smell.
Girls are females, and boys are male.
Everyone says girls are better than boys.
Girls have dolls, and boys have trolls.
Girls can draw, and boys can bite.
And in the end, there's one big fight!

Aimee Auger (8)
Hillbourne Middle School

Summer

The chattering of holidaymakers
as they make their way towards the plane.

The creaking of a deckchair as someone
sits on it.

The blazing sun shining down on people
lying in their deckchairs sleeping.

The whooshing of the waves upon the sand
and bashing against the rocks and boulders.

The sizzling of the burgers on the barbecue
as we all go out there in the summer
with friends and family.

The screams of children swimming and diving
in the sea as the parents relax.

Splat! As a child drops his ice cream on the beach.

But most of all, it's sunny in summer.

James Stacey (10)
Moordown St Johns CE VA Primary School

The Four Seasons

Snowflakes falling to the ground,
White clouds of snow lying daintily on the ground,
Children sitting in front of the warm, crackling fire,
Layer upon layer of ice covering the old garden pond.

New baby lambs being born,
Flowers like daffodils growing in the morning sun,
Bright new green leaves growing on the trees,
April showers flooding everything.

Leaves falling off the trees, orange, yellow and red,
A slight morning breeze drifting through the air,
The smell of something cooking in the oven,
A combine harvester picking the golden corn.

A stroll along the beach,
Playing in the sea to cool us down,
Making sandcastles on the beach,
Sitting along the seafront eating fish and chips.

So now everybody knows why they should not forget
the four seasons!

Rachel Hayes (10)
Moordown St Johns CE VA Primary School

Winter

The cracking of the ice,
And the gushing of the rapid river,
As the crackling fire burns.
The howling of the wind
Thrusting against the window,
And the screeching of the brakes on the ice,
As the snowflakes drop from the sky,
And as the ice cracks underfoot.

Sherrie Hawkins (10)
Moordown St Johns CE VA Primary School

Summer

The laughing of kids building massive sandcastles,
The smash as a surfboard hits the wave,
The sizzling sun high up in the sky burning people down below,
The squeaking of deckchairs when people sit on them,
The whoosh of planes passing by taking people to
                                        sunny destinations,
The screech of a seagull passing by in the bright sky,
The splashing of the waves hitting the sandy shore,
The wail and a splat when a kid drops its ice cream on the beach,
Summer is the time of year when people swim in the deep blue sea.

Katherine Cliff (10)
Moordown St Johns CE VA Primary School

Spring

Baaing of baby lambs as they lie on a
dazzling bed of bright green grass.

The pattering of the April showers
dripping from the open sky
as silent as a tear trickling down a cheek.

A tiny yawn of an animal after its hibernation.

The faint sweet-scented smell of a flower
opening gently like a river flowing.

The humming of the bees collecting pollen
for people to have a sweet taste on their toast.

The deafening crunching sound of the
chocolate Easter egg.

James Fairhall (11)
Moordown St Johns CE VA Primary School

Winter

The cracking of ice as someone slips while skating.
The sneezing of a cold, sick child.
The scraping of the ice skaters' blades on the frozen ice.
The screeching of the brakes of the motor car on ice.
The rustling of the paper being ripped off
Christmas presents by excited children.
The jingle of the snowflakes touching each other.
The whizz of the snowflake as it falls from the sky.
The banging of the fireworks in the moonlit sky.

Benjamin Eyers (10)
Moordown St Johns CE VA Primary School

Spring

The lake unleashes his glass coat,
Mounts of blossom appear on branches,
The layer of snow soaks in and the flowers appear,
The female animals have their babies
And the animal crowds reappear,
Winter gone, summer coming.
Spring!

Jamie Lucas (11)
Moordown St Johns CE VA Primary School

Summer

The shiny glowing sea invites children to play,
And the birds chirp happily in the tall trees,
The scorching sun shines down on the glistening sandcastle
                                          on the shore
As bright, colourful seashells lie out on the grains of yellow sand.

Emma Beale (10)
Moordown St Johns CE VA Primary School

Winter

The crackling of the fire as it burns,
The silence of snowflakes as they fall to the ground.

The laughing of children as they play,
The children are laughing, chucking snowballs at the snowman.

The munching of turkey as people cheer
As they gulp down their drinks.

The blazing fire crackling fiercely,
The thud of Father Christmas' footsteps on the roof.

The popping of party poppers as they spring out for the
'Happy New Year!'

Laura King (10)
Moordown St Johns CE VA Primary School

Summer

People sunbathing in the blazing sun,
Children laughing on the golden sand,
Aeroplanes humming in the clear blue sky,
The buzzing bees going to collect nectar from the bright
                                                colourful flowers,
Children slurping as they lick their cold, white ice creams.

Daniel Hooper (11)
Moordown St Johns CE VA Primary School

Winter

As the howling wind thrusts
against the frosty windowpane,
and as the ice cracks underfoot,
the snowflakes float in the sky,
as the brakes of the car start
to screech as it tries to stop.
Winter is as cold as ice.

Alex Neale (10)
Moordown St Johns CE VA Primary School

The Sounds Of Summer

The roaring of the surfer on his surfboard
as he reaches some gigantic waves.

The blazing sun burning people below
trying to get a tan.

The splashing of children diving into the
swimming pool with their rubber rings.

The zooming of the aeroplane taking
people on the holiday they booked.

The splat of ice cream on the ground.

The sizzling of the sun sitting in the sky
with his sunglasses on.

The squeezing of the suntan bottle.

Summer is the best!

Samuel Beckingham (10)
Moordown St Johns CE VA Primary School

Winter

The crackle of snow as I walk through it,
The screech of a car's wheels as it slides on some ice,
The crash of little children as they slip over in some snow,
The splat of a snowball as it speeds into someone's face,
The thud of a snowman falling to the ground,
The squeal of children as they find it so cold,
The white glittery Christmas tree is filled with bells,
The rattle of bells in a till as people buy presents for everyone,
The cold white snowflakes fluttering down on people,
The scraping of snowboards as they go downhill.

Glenn Innes (11)
Moordown St Johns CE VA Primary School

Autumn

The squawk of birds starting to get cold,
Therefore spreading their wings in a beautiful display
Before migrating to a warmer country
Where the sun shines at this very moment.
The crackling of leaves
As you walk over their dazzling carpet of reds and browns,
As beautiful as a newborn lamb running freely through the fields.
The rustling of paper being ripped frantically off presents,
Like a lion attacking its prey on my birthday.
The horrendous growl of a fearsome bear settling down ready
for hibernation.
The frantic scratch of a rake,
As someone hurries to scoop up all of the beautifully coloured leaves.
What an extravagant and beautiful season autumn is!

Rebecca Hughes (11)
Moordown St Johns CE VA Primary School

Summer Sounds

The brightness of the sun blazing
over people as they get tanned.

The sound of wet feet kicking a football
across the burning sand.

The whooshing of aeroplanes travelling
to faraway countries.

The yells of children splashing
swimming pool water at each other.

The jingle of the ice cream van's song
as it zooms around the corner.

All of these sounds remind me of summer.

Scott Heap (10)
Moordown St Johns CE VA Primary School

Summer

Summer is a scorching time,
When people and holidaymakers
Go to the beach,
It's always a fun time,
But summer is also a busy time.

Summer is a time
When you hear the squirt as a child
Has its suncream put on,
There's mad panic for the last
Few deckchairs at the busy beach,
You hear the wail of a girl
Who has dropped her ice cream,
But most of all you can hear
The screeching of the brakes
As somebody has just missed
A parking space on the cliff top!

Aeroplanes take holidaymakers on holiday,
The fireworks light up the sky
With bangs and crackles,
And the surfboards smack against
The massive waves,
And then the waves roll gently to the shore.

Summer is a scorching time!

Michael Rake (10)
Moordown St Johns CE VA Primary School

Summer

As the children play, summer passes its time.
The chirping birds sing sweetly in the treetops,
The dancing men pat their drums.
The hot sun is shining onto the sea.
People play in the warm water.

Conner Hayes (11)
Moordown St Johns CE VA Primary School

Winter And Summer

Winter
Children wait as they hear the sound of Santa Claus
approaching the chimney, and people of all ages
listen to the Christmas carols.
We look out of our windows and watch the snow fall.
The church bells ring as it's almost Christmas.
But shh! You'll miss Santa!

Summer
I hear the song of the birds when we head down to the beach.
The blazing sun disappears when the moon rises.
Our friends come round to play.
As the sun comes out we start to hear the butterflies
fluttering their wings.

But don't wait too long to see them, it's autumn now!

Amelia Wise (10)
Moordown St Johns CE VA Primary School

Summer

The blazing sun shining right up in the sky,
Burning people below trying to get a tan,
Families having barbecues,
Huge plump sausages sizzling,
Nearly ready to eat from the barbecue.

A splat and a shriek as a little girl drops her strawberry ice cream,
A shiver and a scream of a little boy who has just come out of the sea
And been pecked by a seagull.

Waves crashing against the rocks
And swooping into shore, knocking little children over.

What an extravagant season summer is!

Emily May Scholes (10)
Moordown St Johns CE VA Primary School

Summer

Summer is when love takes place.
Summer is when the heat makes you sticky and hot.
Summer has the sweet tweet of a bird.
Summer smells of flowers, fragrant and bright.
Summer is when lilies come out.
Summer is the opposite to winter.
Summer has the bang of fireworks on Bournemouth beach.
Summer is the bleat of a newborn lamb.
Waves lapping onto the shore.
Buzzing of the bees busily making honey.
In summer there are sizzling barbecues.
The sun settles down for autumn.

Jade Adams (11)
Moordown St Johns CE VA Primary School

Summer Is . . .

Summer is when the children are splashing
and screaming in the swimming pool.

Summer is a child crying because the strawberry
ice cream slid off and went *splat!*

Summer is a child slurping her drink.

Summer is when an ice cream van comes
playing nursery rhyme music.

Summer is a soft moo from a cow.

Summer is a soft puff as a child blows
out the birthday candles.

Tillie Vogt (10)
Moordown St Johns CE VA Primary School

Winter To Summer

Winter

The ice hangs from the warm cosy house,
until it cracks and falls onto the icy cruel ground.
Children scream and shout as the cool snow
hits their warm soft cheeks.
The whispering snowflakes swim through the wind
as it howls through the night.
Children cheer and shout as they wake up to see
a layer of snow covering the ground outside their window.

Summer

Children lick their cold fruity ice lollies
as the snow blows down to the sun and its blaze
hits the coldness.
Children run down to the beach to catch the rushing waves.
The adults sunbathe not knowing of the tricks lurking
nearby under the sand.
So people are having fun all year round!

Amy Cecchinato (11)
Moordown St Johns CE VA Primary School

Spring

The croak of frogs
as they call for mates.

The splashing of streams
flowing down the mountain.

The crack of birds' eggs hatching.

The *baa* of a newborn lamb.

The pitter-patter of the April shower.

Buds popping open all over the ground.

Ashley Metcalf (11)
Moordown St Johns CE VA Primary School

Winter And Summer

Summer is when we can hear the laughing of schoolchildren
Because they have broken up from school,

Winter is when the school kids are shivering inside.

Summer can be as hot as a barbecue,
Winter can be as cold as ice.

Summer is when you can hear the ring of the ice cream van,
Winter is when you can hear carols outside in the bitter cold.

Summer is the time for merry bliss
Winter is a time for Christmas celebration.

The land of winter is blanketed in white cloth but
The land of summer is green and peaceful dreams fill the air.

Frost wrapping on the car on a winter's morn
Glistening sun reflecting in the car mirror all summer's day.

They both have dreams of thick white snow
And the heat of the blinding sun, hotter than ever!

Tasmin Adams (11)
Moordown St Johns CE VA Primary School

Summer And Winter

Summer
The 200mph club speeds down the motorway and
the city is engulfed with the smell of burning rubber.

The whole city is on the beach in their swimming costumes,
sunbathing under the blazing sun.

Winter
Everyone is cooped up in their houses warming themselves
by the fire.

Ice covers the city and all the children are outside
having snowball fights.

Joe Simons (11)
Moordown St Johns CE VA Primary School

The Four Fabulous Seasons

Snowflakes drift through the air and gracefully reach the ground,
Water is enveloped with frozen ice,
And trees are completely bare,
So we shall not forget winter is one of the four seasons.

Summer is a time of constant joy,
There's the splashing waves, screeching seagulls,
And even the slurping of ice cream,
So we shall not forget summer is one of the four seasons.

Leaves take their time to float off trees,
And make a carpet of leaves underfoot,
The frost has descended,
There's a silent breeze,
So we shall not forget autumn is one of the four seasons.

Spring is a month with many celebrations,
For it's a joyful time of year,
There are many flowers,
And lambs are born,
So we shall not forget spring is one of the four seasons.

Jasmine Bell (10)
Moordown St Johns CE VA Primary School

Summer Vs Winter

The buzzing chatter of tourists confused,
The chattering of freezing teeth in the cold,
And laughter rings through the air,
A 'Wow!' as a child opens a present,
A *bang* from the cracker as it bursts
The excitement fades, it's nearly spring,

The 'Ah' as the adult relaxes on the beach,
All the children cry, summer is over,
Back to school, no more fun,
But . . . you see your friends again.

Curtis Sams (10)
Moordown St Johns CE VA Primary School

Sounds Of Summer

Summer is when you hear seagulls squawking.
Summer is when you hear bees making honey.
Summer is when you hear hot dogs sizzling in the sun.
Summer is when you hear children splashing in the sea.

Summer is when you hear crowds of people rushing
                        down to the beach to get a deckchair.
Summer is when you hear a cat on the window sill purring.
Summer is when you hear the soft wind blowing the sea.

Bernadette Bangura (10)
Moordown St Johns CE VA Primary School

Winter

The floating snowflakes from the sky,
And a lake wears a glass coat again.
The sizzling turkey coming out of the oven,
The gushing river going down to the sea.
The howling of the wind thrusting against
                        the frosty windowpane,
As the crackling fire burns against the fireplace,
The thudding of Father Christmas on the roof.

Samuel Clark (10)
Moordown St Johns CE VA Primary School

Winter

The frost crackles underfoot
as the howling wind rushes down the chimney.
The crackling fire burns
as Santa's feet thud on the snow-filled rooftop.
The pattering of raindrops on the window
and the rustling of wrapping paper as children cry with joy.
The silence of the snowflakes drifting in the air
as a coat of ice settles over the puddles.

Alex Nicholls (11)
Moordown St Johns CE VA Primary School

Autumn

The crunch of a fallen leaf underfoot,
A bang and a bash as fireworks stream up into the sky,
I giggle and laugh as trick or treaters collect sweeties,
A howl and a whistle from the wind,
The squeak as the rake is gathering up leaves,
A bark from the dog as thunder begins,
Autumn showers pitter-patter softly,
The waves smack against the rock as autumn gets colder,
Now autumn has come to an end and winter has arrived!

Amy Williamson (11)
Moordown St Johns CE VA Primary School

Summer

Summer is the time when the flowers bloom,
Swaying softly in the gentle breeze.
Summer is the time when hayfever's high,
It makes people sneeze all over the place.
Summer is the time when the sun is boiling,
You go in the sea and your hair gets tangled and mangled.
Summer is the time when children eat ice creams,
Then they drop them on the sand and scream!
I love summer because there's no school.

Sarah Purchase (11)
Moordown St Johns CE VA Primary School

Winter

The silence of the snowflakes swimming through the air
and cracking of ice on the pool,
Crunching of snow on the land.
Diamonds sprayed on the ice but when cracked
they dissolve into nothing.
And a spider's web laced with diamonds.
And the fire is roaring.

Suzy Schindler (10)
Moordown St Johns CE VA Primary School

Winter

The shiver of children
as it begins to snow,

The joy of kids as
they open their presents,

The splat of Santa as he
tumbles down the chimney
and falls into the fireplace,

The shout of the boy who
calls to his mum to come
and look at his snowman,

The cry of the girl who gets
hit by a snowball,

The howl of wolves as they
grow their winter coats.

Jamie Virabi (11)
Moordown St Johns CE VA Primary School

Winter

People slide upon the ice,
Whilst little children squeak because it is too cold.
Mums rush to get last-minute Christmas shopping,
Until the ring of the tills deafens them.
Sitting at home, children gaze out of the window
To see the white carpet of snow,
Hoping that England will turn into a 'snow globe'.
Screeching car brakes piercing my ears.
Teeth-chattering sounds like a tiny hammer
Making a little pop on the wall.
Scraping of ice skaters on the ice
And snow falling everywhere.
What a jolly season winter is.

Emma Bentley (11)
Moordown St Johns CE VA Primary School

Summer And Winter

Summer
Summer is when we can hear the laughing of school kids,
because they've broken up for the school holidays.

You can hear the splashing of swimming pools as we all have fun,
and we are all smelling the sweet smell of daisies and buttercups,
all new and pretty.

Summer is a time when we are all feeling excellent.

Winter
We are all wrapped up tight in warm, woolly clothes and the
bitter rain spits on your face.

Snowflakes silently fall on your car, and you tie your scarf
around your neck.

In winter, we eagerly unwrap our Christmas presents and
scream with delight when we get what we want.

Winter is a chilly but wonderful time of year for us all to enjoy.

Stephanie Nicóla-Miller (11)
Moordown St Johns CE VA Primary School

Autumn

In autumn the leaves turn a golden brown and a flaming red,
The leaves tumble down from the treetops,
The temperature drops and people start to shiver,
And winter draws near,
Families stroll along the sandy, windy beach,
As children ask for ice creams even if they're shivering,
And the next sound you'll hear is a splat and a wail
As a child drops their ice cream in the crunchy wet sand,
But now it is winter, it's started to snow,
And little children shout, 'It's snowing today, hip hip hooray!'
The swirling snowflakes drifting down
Making a crisp white carpet of snow on the frosty pavement,
It will soon be Christmas and St Nicholas will make a visit.

Alice Ryder (10)
Moordown St Johns CE VA Primary School

Winter

Excited children having snowball fights in the white crisp snow.
The crunching of leaves under my feet as I walk through
the thick deep snow.
The ripping and tearing of wrapping paper as you open
your Christmas presents.
The munching and chewing of people eating their scrumptious
Christmas lunch.
The tinkle of a snowflake as it gently hits your cheek.
The pattering of snow as you build a snowman.
The screeching of brakes as the car skids on the ice.

Jack Joyce (10)
Moordown St Johns CE VA Primary School

Summer

People sitting on the beach getting sizzled by the golden sun.
Money jingles as grandparents buy buns.
Children play in the sea.
You can hear the sound of seagulls screeching.
I can hear 'Ah, ahh!' as someone has lost their keys in the sand.
And now everyone says 'Bye' to the beach.

Scott McGarrick (10)
Moordown St Johns CE VA Primary School

Winter

A loud crackle of frost comes from the slippery roof.
Ice slowly melts to clear water.
Bright crisp snow gently flitters to the ground,
As diamonds dance on the frozen lake,
And frost twinkles on the trees.

Thomas Brown (11)
Moordown St Johns CE VA Primary School

Wintertime

The crackling of the fire roaring in the lounge,
The whispering snowflakes falling gently
To make a soft white blanket outside.
The lakes wear a thick coat of solid ice, until *crack!*
The temperature rises.
Tall trees glisten as the wind whistles through their thick branches.
Children shout and scream as snowballs whizz through the air.

Izaak Sedgeley (10)
Moordown St Johns CE VA Primary School

Winter

The crunch of a piece of ice as it breaks,
Fireworks whistling as they race each other up into the dark night sky,
Rustling presents as the paper is ripped off,
Crackers pop as they are pulled,
Waves explode on the hard rocks,
Cars crashing on icy roads,
People skating on lakes of ice,
Bright snowflakes gently flutter down.

Christopher Barrett (10)
Moordown St Johns CE VA Primary School

Silence

Listen to the cement rubbing into the bricks,
The leaves gently falling to the ground.
Hear the swishing wings of the birds,
The worms silently digging their holes,
The laying of the chickens' eggs on the straw.
Hear the planet Mars rotating round,
Hear the clouds passing by.

Lauren Goodwin (8)
Park School

Silence In Your Body

Silence is when you can hear things.
Listen:
Your brain calculating sums,
Fine hair tips lengthening in time,
Or your bones creaking,
To try and move.
Your nails developing
Deep down in the nail bed,
The thumping heartbeat in
Your body,
Or your tummy rapidly churning
When you're worried.
Tummy's digesting food down,
Or your eyes shutting when
You go to bed at night.

Giselle Yonace (8)
Park School

Silence

Silence.
Listen:
The sigh of a bored wall,
Groans from an over-used, worn-out rubber,
The squeaks of pencil sharpenings
As they depart from their pencil friend.
Cries of agony
From the down-trodden floor,
Or the class computer
Crying from the unfairness
Of always having to obey commands.
Electric lights screaming
From the agony of constantly being electrocuted.
No silence.

Timothy Radvan (9)
Park School

Toys In My Bedroom!

I am a doll without any name,
I am a book with no pictures,
The plastic spider in the corner,
The toy cat under the pillow.

I am the hair drier with no cord,
I am the TV without any screen,
The dog in the draw,
The cat in the hat.

I am a pencil with no lead,
I am the scissors that are blunt,
The hamster with no love,
The mouse in the coat pocket.

I am the rabbit in the fridge,
I am the toy baby in the shed,
The dolphin in the closet,
The tiger in the oven.

Lydia Ainsworth (8)
Park School

Tiger

Chasing deer on the marsh,
Swiftly running through the grass.

Treading its lonely desolate tracks,
Its charming colours orange and black.

Being chased by such a dangerous beast,
Could only mean a delicious feast,

Not for you, but only him,
You watch until your life has gone.

The sight of such a mighty beast
Could only mean - tiger!

Henry Turner (11)
Park School

Happy Animals!

I am the lamb with the warm wool,
I am the rabbit with the jolly bounce,
I am the horse with the deafening neigh,
The cow with the black spots,
The dog with the frightful yap!

I am the cat with the delightful purr,
I am the hamster with the scampering feet,
I am the bird carrying my food to my nest,
The ladybird with the three black spots,
The snake with the slithery skin!

Abigail Coward (9)
Park School

Complete Silence

Everyone, complete silence please,
Listen very carefully.
Can you hear the whisper of
A cat's whisker,
The swing of a spider's web,
A blink of an eye,
The crying of the wind,
Can you hear the sun rising
Or a flower dying?

James Sidwick (8)
Park School

I Am . . .

I am the queen without any make-up,
I am the shiny nail without pink varnish,
I am the pink and silver necklace without the neck,
And the sparkling earring with no ear,
The short skirt without long legs,
And a boot without a heel.

Eloise Dudley (9)
Park School

Listen

There is a silence,
Listen:
Clouds proceed into place,
Sands moving,
Birds soaring up above,
The wind in the sky,
And a stick trailing along the ground,
Fish swimming in the water,
And last . . .
The oxygen . . .
Everywhere.

Ava Hawkins (9)
Park School

I Am . . .

I am the anaconda with no wrap,
The lizard with no tail,
The bee with no sting,
I am the dragon with no fire.

I am the skunk with no smell,
I am a turtle with no shell,
The bull with no horns.

Karl Al-Omar (8)
Park School

Listen

Listening is when you hear things,
So listen:
You can hear the giggling of a teddy,
The jumping of a jumping jack,
A doll that is cleaning,
And a toy kitty's purr.

Daniel Couto-Poci (9)
Park School

Teachers Are Hound Dogs

Teachers are hound dogs,
They patrol the corridors,
Barking when it's playtime,
'Who disobeys the rules?'

Sniffing out the culprit,
Scratching at the doors,
Howling after school time,
'Who dares to still be at school?'

Never ever smiling,
Always got the grumps,
Slobbering when it's lunchtime,
'Who breaks the silent rule?'

Sniffing and snooping,
Scratching and shouting,
Growling at class time,
'How dare you write this poem?'

Sophie Watton (10)
Park School

I Am . . .

I am the jumper without any thread
I am the window without any glass
I am the Game Boy without any game
I am the tree without any leaves
I am the clock without any numbers

I am sad!

I am the board pen without any board
I am the teacher without any children
I am the child without any parents
I am the printer without any paper
I am the boy without any name

I am sad!

Dominic Lees-Bell (8)
Park School

The Park

Here the leaves are green,
The flowers bright in bloom,
Here the birds are humming,
The children are playing zoom,
This place is playful, it is the park.

Everyone's gone home now,
The animals are coming out,
There is a fox as red as a rose,
It is also as white as a dove,
This place is quiet, it is the park.

Here the leaves are falling down,
The children kick the leaves,
All the animals are going to sleep,
The leaves are yellow and brown,
This place is bare, it is the park.

All the leaves are gone now,
The children are not here,
Here Mother Nature is fast asleep,
Only to awake in spring,
This place is dead, it is the park.

Ryan Crooks (10)
Park School

I Am . . .

I am the jellyfish without a sting,
I am a car without any petrol,
I am a ruler snapped in half.

I am a crab without any home,
Trousers without a belt,
A man being captured.

I am a bullet being fired,
A pen without any ink,
A man without a friend.

Ryan Frankel (8)
Park School

Looking Through My Window

I stand here gazing through a window
And there is a messy table.
Around the table are chairs.
A cat is sleeping on one.

Chloe Keefe Barton (9)
Portesham Primary School

Flowers

Flowers are beautiful,
Flowers are colourful,
Flowers are wonderful
And people like big bunches.

Louise Morris (9)
Portesham Primary School

The Butterfly

Round and round the garden they go,
Buttering their fingers as they flow.
Landing on the flowers,
Using their powers,
Off they hop popity-pop
Landing on the flowerpot.

Chloe Snuggs (10)
Portesham Primary School

I Love

I love the trees swaying in the wind
And the streams flowing down the hills
And the sunset sky going down
For the stars to shine all night long.

Daniel Burnett (10)
Portesham Primary School

The Toucan

In the big jungle
Lives a lively little bird.
Squawking happily
With his lively little friends;
Pecking with their colourful beaks.

Adam Snape (10)
Portesham Primary School

Monkey

I like making noise,
I like to tell people jokes,
I have a long tail,
I only walk on two legs,
I like swinging in big trees.

Jack Taylor (11)
Portesham Primary School

My Bedroom Tanka

My bedroom I have
Is as cosy as can be.
My bed I lie in
Dreaming as I sleep all night
Reading before *I shut up!*

Sian Hennessy (10)
Portesham Primary School

I See Outside

I see the trees blow,
There are people walking by.
I hear the birds sing,
As rain drips down the window.

Rachel Mayo (10)
Portesham Primary School

Snowflakes

Snowflakes fall down
Like a cold gown.
When the sun comes
Hummingbirds hum.
Children like to play
In it all day
And build snowmen
While forgetting to feed the hen.
I love snow
I blow and blow and blow
And the lake freezes,
There are slight breezes.
On the green tree are glistening flakes
Oh yeah, and I love skating on iced lakes.

Livia Peterkin (9)
Portesham Primary School

Kennings School

Lunch-muncher
Ball-puncture
Test-teacher
Crisp-cruncher
Head teacher
Book-reader
Football-chaser
Football-teacher
Cool-learner
Bunsen burner
Homework-setter
Ball-hitter
Assembly-leader
Basketball-teacher.

Charlotte Barlow (10)
Portesham Primary School

What's Behind The Door?

(Based on 'The Door' by Mirostav Holub)

What's behind the door?
Shall I go and open it?
Maybe there is an island or a haunted house,
Or an old man looking for his mouse.

What's behind the door?
Shall I go and open it?
Maybe there's a wood or a nursery school
With lots of children and a juggler called Paul.

What's behind the door?
Shall I go and open it?
Maybe there's a different land like outer space
Or there is a shop full of sweets or my mum's place.

Chloe Mackenzie (7)
Portesham Primary School

Beyond The Door

(Based on 'The Door' by Mirostav Holub)

Beyond the door
lies Chocolate Land.
Everything is chocolate,
even chocolate sand.

Beyond the door
is there Sweetie Country?
Are the books made of sweets?
Are the books munchy?

Beyond the door
will there be a place with no school?
That would be great,
there might be a pool!

Beyond the door
there could just be a door
or maybe just an apple core.

Ellena Minns (9)
Portesham Primary School

Beyond The Door

(Based on 'The Door' by Mirostav Holub)

Beyond the door,
Maybe there are slaves
Who are poor . . .

Or
Squishy-squashy, spongy land
Where the giant sponge
Might still stand.

A haunted house
With a graveyard that surrounds.
A massive party,
Very annoying for people
In their nightgowns.

Is that what's beyond the door?
Let's go and see,
Shall we?

Crrreak!
It opened!
Look inside!
Oh it's just a cupboard!

Anna Freiesleben (9)
Portesham Primary School

Enjoy The Earth

Enjoy the Earth, enjoy the sky,
Enjoy all the things that fly.

Enjoy the Earth, enjoy the camels,
Enjoy all the mammals.

Enjoy the Earth, enjoy the sea,
Enjoy all the things that swim like me.

Enjoy the Earth for it is precious.

Lee Thomas Williamson (9)
Portesham Primary School

Beyond The Door

(Based on 'The Door' by Mirostav Holub)

Is there a war beyond the door?
No, but there might be technical land.

Is there a war beyond the door?
No, but it might lead to a party in Hawaii.

Is there a war beyond the door?
No but there might be Popcorn Land.
Who knows? I don't.

Is there a war beyond the door?
No, but there might be a different dimension.

Is there a war beyond the door?
No, but there might be a sweet shop.

Is there a war beyond the door?
No, but there might be shark-infested custard.

Is there a war beyond the door?
For the last time *no!*

Maisie Dean (7)
Portesham Primary School

Beyond The Door

(Based on 'The Door' by Mirostav Holub)

Go and open the door
Maybe outside there's a city made of chocolate and sweets
Or a faraway island.

Go and open the door
Maybe there's a river sparkling with gold
Or maybe a secret garden.

Go and open the door
Maybe there's a palace made of gold, silver and jewels
Or a magic city.

Just go and open the door.

Molly Booker (7)
Portesham Primary School

Go And Open The Door

(Based on 'The Door' by Mirostav Holub)

Go and open the door,
Maybe there's six ladies
Or ten babies.

Go and open the door,
Maybe there's a house
Or a mouse.

Go and open the door,
Maybe there's a pop band
Or a magic land.

Go and open the door,
Maybe there's a manky
Old hankie.

Go and open the door,
Maybe there's a panel
Or an animal.

Go and open the door,
Maybe there's a sink
That is pink.

Go and open the door,
Maybe there's a deer
With no earl.

Maybe there's a cow,
You might not know
What's beyond the door.

Meredith Harman (9)
Portesham Primary School

What's Behind The Door?

(Based on 'The Door' by Mirostav Holub)

Go and open the door!
Better go and open it.
There might be cats near the window
Or there might be dogs barking.
So go and open the door!

Go and open the door!
There might be ladies talking in the street,
There might be elephants charging.
So go and open the door!

Go and open the door!
There might be sirens going,
There might be the sound of engines in the street.
So go and open the door!

Go and open the door!
There might be a haunted house
With spiders everywhere.
Go and open the door!

Go and open the door!
There might be the sound of music,
There might be the sound of screaming.
Go and open the door.

Go and open the door!
There might be Chocolate Land.
You won't know until
You go and open the door!

Katie Wilson (9)
Portesham Primary School

The Door
(Based on 'The Door' by Mirostav Holub)

Go and look behind the door,
Maybe outside there's a land of bees or trees,
Or someone killing or swimming.

Go and look behind the door,
Maybe there's a cool person,
Or a pool.

Go and look behind the door,
Outside there's a kitten, or a mitten,
Or grapes, or apes.

At least there might be a puppet show!

Amy Taylor (8)
Portesham Primary School

The View Inside

From outside I see
the inviting warm fire
staring back at me.
My family sit around
relaxing, watching TV.

Lisa Robinson (9)
Portesham Primary School

Praying Mantis Tanka

Gorgeous, but deadly
killer waiting for its prey
and saying its grace.
First it sucks its prey's nice blood
then it slices it all up.

Daniel Jones (11)
Portesham Primary School

Beyond The Door
(Based on 'The Door' by Mirostav Holub)

Shall we see what's beyond the door?

Maybe there's a pen click-clicking
Or a robber nick-nicking.

Maybe there's a bus vroom, vrooming
And a lorry broom-brooming.

Maybe there's a rabbit jump-jumping
Or some bad boys thump-thumping.

Come on let's go and open the door.
Wow! It's only the garden shed.

Abigail Booker (8)
Portesham Primary School

The Beach

I am very empty,
Wind whipping sand from me,
The water is cold,
The jellyfish are stinging,
The fish are going crazy.

Matthew Alvis (9)
Portesham Primary School

The Kitchen

Sharp knives are flashing,
Cupboard doors opening,
Dinner plates waiting,
The cups are drinking coffee,
The clean floor is beautiful.

Robert Harrington (10)
Portesham Primary School

Beyond The Door

(Based on 'The Door' by Mirostav Holub)

Go and pull open the door!
Maybe there will be a haunted house,
Planet Hero or an enchanted wood.

Go and pull open the door!
Maybe there will be a ghostly forest,
A windswept castle or a dock with ships.

Go and pull open the door!
Maybe there will be an empty sea,
A myth-made Earth or a treasure island.

Jack Bellworthy (7)
Portesham Primary School

Bedtime Hour

Darkness is all around me,
while I'm lying in my bed.
The landing light is on
and it's shining on my head.

I shut my eyes tight,
and try to think of something
but I feel all funny
so I think of a big diamond ring.

Laura Croxson (10)
Portesham Primary School

In My Living Room

In my living room
I see the lovely fire.
In my chair I sit,
Watching its flames flick higher.
I chill out watching TV.

Scarlet Moon (11)
Portesham Primary School

Celebrate Your World

I celebrate the sight
of the roaring sea, crashing
against the huge rocks.

I celebrate the sound
of the soft wind, the sound of
my cats purring
and the sound of my harp.

I celebrate the sweet taste
of orange juice and
delicious apples.

I celebrate the feel
of soft blue velvet on an
old dress.

I celebrate the memory
of my carriage pony
and what a life she had.

Charlotte Sutton (9)
Port Regis School

The Man From The Moon

There upon a cliff lies a castle from a myth
Approach it as you shall
Be wary is my will
For around the castle there lies a moat
And a boat
A very mysterious one too
For there lies an old man with a straw hat
He sits there smoking his pipe
Till his pipe turns blue
There he sings his song
With the stars around him
He smiles
And disappears into the moon.

Edward Macdonald (8)
Port Regis School

Celebrate Your World

I celebrate
The sight of the dark forest.
The animals crawling like caterpillars
Finding some food.

I celebrate
The sound of lovely music,
And a girl dancing like a ballerina
On the stage.

I celebrate
The feel of sleeping on the grass,
The sun shining on me
With lovely weather.

I celebrate
The taste of the apples.
The fresh juice coming out.
Everybody looking for them
In the supermarket.

I celebrate
The memory of good dreams.
I have a really big house
With ten bedrooms
In the middle of the sea.

Zeta Leung (9)
Port Regis School

My Brother And Sister

My sister is as annoying as a leaking roof!
My brother is as fast as a Komodo dragon.
My brother is as friendly as a cocker spaniel.
My sister talks for hours!
My brother thinks like the spellchecker on the computer.
My brother's hands are like ice.
My sister reacts like a dramatic octopus!

Patrick Milne (9)
Port Regis School

Young Writers - Once Upon A Rhyme Dorset

A River Of Lava

A river of lava flows as fast as rapids coming towards a waterfall.
The suffocating smoke wraps around me like a snake coiling
round its prey.
The lava fountain belches out red-hot, fiery cinders and burning rock.
It sounds as if the Devil is lurking in the mountain,
Growling, grumbling and roaring,
Exploding at this very moment.
The trees bow down to the flowing lava, as it rushes down
the mountain,
Hissing at every living thing
And spitting its fiery venom like a dragon scorching a path across
the land.
It devours the landscape
Until, satisfied, it rests
Waiting for the moment to hunt again.

Flora McFarlane (9)
Port Regis School

Caves

Inside the cave it's eerie, as the freezing air runs down the back
of your spine,
The dark, damp rocks shaped like ghostly fantastic demons, stare up
at you like shadowy monsters.
The slimy wall stands patiently as the moss eats away at the rock.
The ceiling is so low
The cave is cramped and silent
Apart from the
drip,
drip,
drip
of the water from the jaggedy ceiling.

Jack Gething (8)
Port Regis School

Snow

I woke up one morning
To find the emerald green grass had turned to milky-white.
I put my red woolly mittens on
And ran to the back door *whoosh!*
The great breeze fell into me.
I forced myself to move forward.
I went through the door to find white shapes falling from the sky.
The ground had a big, white sheet over it.
I picked the white sheet up
And the beautiful sheet fell to bits.
I looked to see if any other places had this beautiful, pearly sheet
Yes, they had.
The shapes started to fall faster.
I caught one and held it tight in my hand.
Then I uncurled my fingers
Nothing was there!
Then I got another and another.
They were like diamonds falling from the sky.
I decided to go inside
But to remind me,
I would take some of this pearly white cover.

The next morning,
I looked out of my window
It had all gone.

I looked in my pocket
It was gone, too.

Oh well,
Maybe next year it will come again.

Anna Gray (8)
Port Regis School

Riding On A Dragonfly

I was riding on a dragonfly,
My hair rushing through the wind.
The dragonfly's wings shimmered like glass
They had tiny little sparkles of glitter in them.
I was flying over the Antarctic and the Mediterranean Sea.
I sailed over Everest
I even think I saw the Ancient Greek gods on Mount Olympus.
I fluttered over Africa
Where the king of the animals lives - the lion.
His roar was so loud the whole continent trembled.
I flew to the end of the rainbow
Where I met Dorothy and Toto
I got my bag of golden treasure.

Back in my room
I gazed at the dragonfly
Sketched in twinkling stars
Over the velvet sky.

Elizabeth Killick (8)
Port Regis School

I Wish, I Wish, I Wish

I wish my hair was straight.
I wish I could spin around the world like a radiant bauble.
I wish I was really adorable.

I wish I could climb trees like a chimpanzee in the zoo.
I wish I had a diamond ring that sparkled in the light.
I wish my pony was magical and could fly.
I wish my brother could sing like Robbie Williams.
I wish I was older than eight.

Scarlett Aichroth (8)
Port Regis School

Snow

Through my window the snow gleamed brightly in the morning sun.
It invited me to go out and play.
I built a snowman with a carrot for a nose.
He watched me while I played in the soft and powdery snow.
My fingers felt cold and tingly.
I wanted him to join the fun
But he only smiled as I played alone.

The light shining through the windows reminded me it was teatime
So I rushed inside
My fingers burning with the heat.

Through my window, the next morning, I saw the snow had gone.
All that was left of my snowman was a puddle.

Sophie Cahill (8)
Port Regis School

My Snowman

Snowmen with their cold, snowy bodies,
Snowmen with their flat caps on their snowy, round heads.
Snowmen with their carrot noses,
Snowmen with their warm scarves,
Snowmen with their stick arms.
Next morning I woke up
All that was left was
A hat,
A carrot
And a scarf!

I ran outside and made another one.
I danced around it all day
Until it was dark.
I said my goodbyes and ran inside.

Emily Matthews (9)
Port Regis School

Celebrate Your World

I celebrate
The sight of tulips
Blowing in the wind
Their rustling petals.

I celebrate
The sound of crackling lamb,
In the oven
Cooking.

I celebrate
The feel of snow
Blowing on my cold face
In the
Winter breeze.

I celebrate
The taste of an
Ice lolly tingling
On my
Teeth.

I celebrate
The memory
Of myself
Swimming with the
Fishes under the sea.

George Butler (10)
Port Regis School

Haiku

The lazy tortoise
Trudged slowly onwards through the
Slimy, gooey mud.

Freddy Bunbury (11)
Port Regis School

A Place On The Other Side
Of The World

Yesterday I went to the zoo,
And I saw a fat kangaroo.
He bounced up and down
His tail swirled around and around.
Next he said, 'How do you do?'

Today it was sunny
And I thought it was funny,
Because I saw a toad
Being dragged by a bunny.

Tomorrow I'm going out with my mum,
And she has a very big bum.
I'm going to stroke a leopard
While she is in a café drinking rum.

Jazz Bisset (10)
Port Regis School

My Baby Brother

My baby brother is as swift as a hare,
And as handsome as a prince.

My baby brother is as playful as a puppy,
And reacts like a lion . . . He bites!

My baby brother is as loud as a volcano,
And behaves like a monkey.

My baby brother talks like an alien from outer space,
And walks like a stick insect.

My baby brother's hands are like monsters
Coming to grab you,
And take you into his wooden jail (cot)!

Jamie Horton (8)
Port Regis School

At The Seaside

Ice creams melt
Sandcastles grow high.
People are swimming and
Bodies lie bathing.
Beach huts are opened and
Everyone comes to the beach
On a hot summer's day.

The sea becomes vicious
And rain spits stones at my face.
The wind howls like a wolf,
And lightning and thunder fight.
Rock pools are left and
Shells not picked up.
Beach huts are all closed
On a cold winter's day.

Lizzie Potts (11)
Port Regis School

Christmas Stocking

Lots of presents sticking out
Christmas feeling all about!
Squeeze it,
Feel it,
Rattle it around,
Listen to the stocking sound!
So exciting,
Aching to see,
This Christmas
Stocking is
Taunting me.

Gabriel Dorey (9)
Port Regis School

A Dead World

The world was ruined,
There was fire everywhere, the woods were burning.
Trees were falling down,
I didn't know what to do.
There were animals being shot,
They were falling to the floor,
War was happening in other countries
It was horrible.
The ground was dark with soil and no flowers,
The sky was grey and grotty,
Soil was flying everywhere hitting people in the face.
I thought the world was *dead!*

Eliza Hamer (10)
Port Regis School

A Beautiful Creature

Prancing round in the field,
Whenever are they going to stop.

Galloping through the woods,
The beautiful creatures pass me.

Rearing up in the air,
Up I watch their front two hooves go.

Calling to their friends,
Their tails swishing in the wind.

The smell of the wild creatures' breath,
Hitting me with warmth.

They're still prancing round the field,
I wonder whether they'll stop.

Eloise Smail (11)
Port Regis School

My Imagination For A New Generation

My imagination for a new generation is
Four-legged cars called Jaguars.

My imagination for a new generation is
A homework machine with an invisible screen.

My imagination for a new generation is
An ozone mender or a pet-robot vendor.

My imagination for a new generation is
A robot tooth brusher or an elder sister crusher.

My imagination for a new generation is
A time machine or a teacher who is not mean!

Toby Mather (10)
Port Regis School

Kennings Monkeys

Nut-droppers,
Lunatic-laughers,
Tree-treckers,
Cheerful-chatterers.

Crazy-climbers,
Boisterous-bickerers,
Annoying-arguers,
Disobedient-daredevils.

Playful-players,
Mischievous-misbehavers,
Forest-friends,
Jolly-jokers.

They are:
Cheeky monkeys!

Amy Watson (10)
Port Regis School

Promise Of Friendship

I want to be friends with you
Till we are a
Million years old,
Till aliens take over the world
And the sky freezes and leaves turn white.

If we are friends
I will let you have my 1000 colour biro
And let you stand
In front of me
In the moon ride.

I will give you
The sweetest of toffees
The wisdom of Jupiter's rays
And my last Yu-Gi-Oh deck.

I will like you more than
My pet goldfish in the bowl
The way ripples whisper
And a Twix chocolate bar.

Wil Milligan (10)
Port Regis School

My Beaver Cousin

My beaver cousin,
Busy and energetic,
Builds lots of things
Full of energy, he jumps all about.
He builds lots of dens
To store his food.

Jack Deverell (8)
Port Regis School

The Strange Dream

Singing is my love, my life, my sunshine,
But he brought bitter death to my heart.
They laugh and shout, for there is no
More languid music in my heart.
But who are they?
Where are they?
Hot blood runs through my veins,
A black shadow surrounds me and a
Sad scream fills my heart.
I open my mouth to sing but there is only a
Weak moan, my voice, my symphony of
Power has abandoned me.
In the purple sky the enormous moon looks
Down at me and the storm whispers
The sea wind wraps around me and I fall
Into cool sleep.
But my dreams trouble me too.
The ships of the water are no more.
The rocks are covered in mermaids singing.
I awake, with my head full of jealousy of their voice.
But why can't I sing?
I tried once more and my own voice
Echoes through my mouth.
It was a dream, a strange dream,
A taunting dream, a mocking dream
But a dream to remember.

Madeleine Vaughan (10)
Port Regis School

My Penguin Dad

My penguin dad he's smart and smooth,
He gobbles up his food in a flash.
He waddles everywhere and cares a lot for me,
He keeps me warm every day,
A torpedo in the water.

Lloyd Wallace (8)
Port Regis School

Inside My Head

There is a football
That I always kick around,
And a friend to do headers with.

A crazy dip that fizzes rapidly in your mouth
And the occasional refresher on Saturdays and Wednesdays.
The taste of chewing off the lollipop stick.

People flying instead of walking,
No lessons to attend,
And eternal life.

Sprout wings, fly away and live a life of your own,
Run at the speed of light and jump into the sky.
Slide down rainbows and land in a pool of tuck,
Speed out of Earth and onto Mars.

Be American and make friends with a pizza,
Go to the cinema all day with unlimited Coke,
Destroy each single Yu-Gi-Oh card on Earth -
Even the fake ones and the printed ones.

Chris Pudner (11)
Port Regis School

My Doggy Dad

My doggy dad lies around all day,
Grooming his coat.
When he's angry,
He barks at me.
When he is happy,
He plays ball with me.
He never gets tired
And is always there for me.

Alex Sage (10)
Port Regis School

The Rugby World Cup

The tension is rising,
The stadium was packed,
As the two teams ran on,
The crowd rose,
Cheered and clapped.

Australia were winning,
But we fought back,
With the ball always spinning,
We strengthened our pack.

England were in front,
By not very much!
Conditions were miserable,
But our boys were tough.

Conversions and a try,
Made our spirits high,
As the final whistle blew,
We all knew,
With the score 14 all,
Now was our cue.

Into extra time,
When . . .
Jonny Wilkinson had his prime,
He kicked the ball,
It sailed over the pole,
With a large uproar,
We had scored!

We had won the ultimate prize,
And Johnson held the trophy high,
Moments to treasure,
Memoirs to favour,
For the first time the Webb Ellis trophy,
Was ours to savour!

Philippa Kerby (10)
Port Regis School

My Monkey Brother

My monkey brother
Acts crazy every day.
Swinging from tree to tree.
Playing menacingly around the house.
Chattering with his friends,
While bouncing on his bed
And gobbling up his sweets
Before Mum can see.

Timothy Dickens (8)
Port Regis School

My Eagle Gran

My gran, my eagle gran,
Is a terror!
With her beady eyes
She stands there proudly
In the mist of the night.
She swoops down on me
When she is cross.
She is frightening,
My eagle gran.

Kathryn Francis (8)
Port Regis School

My Lion Brother

My lion brother
Is very proud.
He's always pleased with himself.
He gnaws his food, smacking his lips
Roaring in anger when I annoy him.

Anders Horwood (8)
Port Regis School

My Snake Dad

My snake dad
Is the crafty one.
Smooth and gentle,
He slithers and slides
Around the house,
Quietly finishing off his work.
Lazing and relaxing
In the sun.
When he's happy he rattles
And when he's sad he hisses.

Joseph Tuersley (8)
Port Regis School

My Owl Cousin

My cousin Caspar is like an owl.
Bright, beady eyes,
Wise and quiet
And very inquisitive.
He loves staying up at night
And hides wearily during the day.

Benedict Judd (8)
Port Regis School

My Pig Brother

He grunts when he's sad,
He squeals when he's happy.
He rolls in the mud.
He's greedy and gobbles his food in one go.

James Pullen (8)
Port Regis School

Hate And Joy

Hate
Hate is grey like a dark cloud blocking out all light,
It smells like smouldering ash in the eye of darkness,
Hate tastes like oil killing everything in the ocean of goodness,
It sounds like chalk on a blackboard blocking out the sound of life,
It feels like a cold sword stabbing at your heart,
Hate lives in the very heart of blackness.

Joy
Joy is gold like the sun which brings us the good things in life,
It smells like lavender bringing beautiful smells into the garden,
Joy tastes like honey tickling your throat,
It sounds like a bluebird singing its sweet song of life,
It feels like silky feathers from the bird of joy,
Joy lives in the well of joy.

Chloe Jacout (9)
Port Regis School

The Kingfisher

An azure streak glints in the sun,
As he surges across the sky,
Landing on an old dead branch,
Above the aquamarine river.
His form so beautiful,
Breast and under-wing so bronze.
The wonderful russet
Blends into the sapphire blue
From breast to wing.
Full of life, full of power,
Its speckled head as still as the sun.
He sits on the branch
Watching the flowing river.
Strollers stare as the kingfisher is set alight
As he explodes into a dive
Falling like a missile.

Marcus Willis (11)
Port Regis School

Promise Of Friendship

I want to be friends with you
Till we die
Till the petals fall off the flowers
And till the world has collapsed.

If we are friends
I will play with you
And I will laugh with you
And not let anything come between us,

I will give you
A fresh beginning to a good friendship
And a happy ending to your life
And my last pack of crisps.

I will like you more than
The first snowflake that falls in my mouth
And more than my bunny rabbits.

Natasha Collins (10)
Port Regis School

Ice

A stinging wind
Weaves a web of ice
Strangling plants,
In their sleep.
The wind's teeth bite
Into delicate leaves
Trailing icy saliva.
Spears of grass glint,
With sharp ivory points;
Piercing the freezing air.

Alistair John Hughes (11)
Port Regis School

Promise Of Friendship

I want to be friends with you till we are reborn in a new world
And our candles of life have melted.

If we are friends
I will give you brightness of gold
And give you my favourite toy.

I will visit your grave, even when you are gone
And mourn at it.

I will give you
The goodness of the world's people
And let you have my favourite sticks.

I will like you more than history lessons
And my own bedroom.

Cameron Mackie (9)
Port Regis School

Pomegranate

Outside an oddly shaped globe
Like a lightbulb
Covered in two different colours
Remembrance of autumn.

Inside is the treasure
Hidden by the dull apple-like interior
Pink seeds grow like rubies
Each seed in its own pink globe
Like Matrioshka, neatly packed globes in their own
Big globe.

Bridget Harris (11)
Port Regis School

Love And Hate

Love
Love is reddy pink,
It smells like flowers in bloom.
Love tastes like strawberries with sugar and cream,
It was quiet, peaceful and pure,
It feels soft, happy and squidgy,
Love lives in people, somewhere . . . special.

Hate
Hate is red,
It smells like hot rhubarb straight from the oven,
It tastes like Tabasco sauce,
Hate sounds like a rude words competition,
It feels hot and sharp,
Hate lives in fire.

Christopher Brinkworth (10)
Port Regis School

The Kingfisher

As the sun rises, the burnished kingfisher sits
The dazzling glisten of colours glints in the sun,
The strong, sharp beak waits for his prey,
A still chestnut figure.
Suddenly a streak of flashing colours swoop through the air,
A glow of turquoise wings
Following the sun
Crashes into the glass
Breaking its neck.
The beautiful frame lies still.
He will not see another dawn.

Harriet Hedges (9)
Port Regis School

The Dream

He walks through the window
He opens your ear
He takes a step in,
It's a dream.

He finds a seat
At the back of your head
And opens his suitcase
He begins his work
It's a dream.

You and I dream
While he works
Typing and thinking
That's all he does.

It's a dream,
It's a dream,
Goodnight!

Lucy Lloyd-Williams (11)
Port Regis School

Fairies

Fairies, fairies, dance at night,
Under the moonlight,
With their dazzle of
Twinkling dust.
Where they dance at night.
They ice skate on the frozen water,
That's what fairies do at night.

Daisy Kerby (7)
Port Regis School

Abstract Nouns

Hope
Hope is yellow
It smells like freshly opened rose petals,
Hope tastes like lemons and honey,
It sounds like fluttering wings,
It feels warm and smooth,
Hope lives at the end of a dark tunnel.

Disappointment
Disappointment is grey,
It smells like smoke,
Disappointment tastes salty,
It sounds like teardrops on a stone floor,
It feels wet and cold,
Disappointment lives at the end of a phone call.

Saskia Tempest-Radford (10)
Port Regis School

A Pair Of Poems

Hate
Hate is red as blood,
It smells like melting plastic,
It tastes as sour as a lemon,
Hate sounds like rocks splitting in two,
It feels strong and sharp like a sword,
Hate lives in the epicentre of an earthquake.

Peace
Peace is as white and blue as the sky,
It smells like tulips and daffodils,
It tastes as sweet as honey,
Peace sounds like music in the hills,
It feels as soft as wool,
Peace lives in Heaven.

Lara Good (9)
Port Regis School

10 Things Found In Willy Wonka's Pocket

The smell of everlasting gobstoppers wafting through the air,
A scrumdidilyumptious bar of chocolate,
A new piece of chocolate to be tested by children,
A strip of wallpaper candy,
A boat ticket to Oompah Loompa land,
Some cocoa beans for the Oompah Loompas,
A list of things he needs for the chocolate garden,
The names of people who have won Golden Tickets,
Half of a pocket watch,
The one ingredient that will make tastebuds go
Boom!

Samantha Pearce (11)
Port Regis School

Flame

It is like a snake wandering,
It is a head looking for something it has lost,
The flame dances in the dark,
The flame is like a person, it can wither or grow tall,
The flame is so beautiful but so deadly,
It is like a sparkler in the wind,
It is a multicoloured pattern,
It is like a coiled viper,
The flame can give life or death.

Jack Ruddy (9)
Port Regis School

Haiku On 'Kensuke's Kingdom'
By Michael Morpurgo

Falling from a boat
Luckily alive and safe
Stuck on an island.

Patrick Allen (11)
Port Regis School

Haiku

Dragon's fiery curse,
Scorches and burns land in sight,
Goes dormant again.

Max Austin-Little (10)
Port Regis School

Haiku

Paper lanterns sway
Gleaming in the midnight sky
A Chinese wonder!

Nick Meares (11)
Port Regis School

Pets

A dog is surely man's best friend,
Perhaps the most popular of pets,
He is loyal and loving to the very end,
But how he hates the vet's!

A cat will purr his way into your heart,
Yes this pet is surely a winner,
But he'll leave you when he wants to depart,
But be sure he'll be back for his dinner!

A budgie, a sweet and colourful bird,
Who sits in his cage and sometimes he talks,
He chirps and cheeps all day, he can be heard,
Except on a bad day he squawks.

To groom and to love and to ride in the sun,
A little girl's dream is a pony,
Weekends and summer days would be so much fun,
I can hear the signs now. *If only.*

Hazel Goldman (10)
St Mary's CE Primary School, Bridport

Dolphins

All the dolphins jumping around,
Leaping through the ocean,
Never touching the world's dry ground,
With the waves and their swirly motion.

The jumping dolphins in the sea,
People see them happy as can be,
I have not met a porpoise yet,
As they are dying in the fisherman's net.

All the dolphins jumping around,
Splashing through the ocean,
Sometimes touching the ocean ground,
With the waves and their foamy lotion.

The dolphins blue and white,
Swim away out of sight.

Billie Goldman (10)
St Mary's CE Primary School, Bridport

Roses

You can feel rose scent
Running through your veins.

It conjures up happy memories
Of wonderful places, faces and names.

You can feel the softness of their petals
When you rub them between your fingers.

Lauren Ford (9)
St Mary's CE Primary School, Bridport

Perfect

The light is here
The night is clear

The day has dawned
It's early morn

Tomorrow has gone
For evermore
And now the light breaks through
The open door

I wish that people would think before
They judged each other by their skin colour

If we could live in a perfect world
If it were me
Then it would mean

No wars or people getting hurt

More charities like NCH

No lies or cheats

And lots more people to meet

Every night I dream of that and know
That more people like me could make it happen
And let other people have
A chance to speak!

Amica Dickson (9)
St Mary's CE Primary School, Bridport

Dolphins

The jumping dolphins in the sea,
The people see them happy as can be,
I don't see the dolphins so often now as it is winter.
The sea is rough and cold.
The dolphins blue and white swim away out of sight.

Louise Bottle (10)
St Mary's CE Primary School, Bridport

My Best Friend

Me and my best friend Billy,
Like playing on the PlayStation,
Billy goes very silly,
When we play for the nation.

Billy likes playing football,
Even when his feet are sore,
Even when it is so cold,
He still goes on more and more.

When I'm ill he comes over,
We play on the Nintendo,
And we go undercover,
We play with squishy Play'Doh.

He is my friend for evermore,
Even when we beat each other up,
I help him up when he is sore,
We will be friends when we grow up.

Leif Sanders (10)
St Michael's CE VA Primary School, Lyme Regis

My Friend

One day I met my friend
She was quite a lot of fun,
She said 'She will always
Be around,' we went to the
Beach in the sun!

We are having a lot of fun,
But now our time is nearly done,
Stay away, stay around
But you will always be found.

I will see you in the dark,
I will see you in the park,
And I will always see you at the weekend.

Samantha Bird (9)
St Michael's CE VA Primary School, Lyme Regis

Nature's War

Then soldiers came and cut down the trees,
They almost killed ten hundred bees,
They left the forest and went into the wood,
Surely they meant no good.

They where killing nature and all its fish,
How could they be so foolish?
Nature had to fight back,
Wolves, bears, great cats arranged an attack.

They would be ambushed at the pear trees,
The commanders were intelligent monkeys,
The soldiers came and went to the pear trees,
But suddenly they all got stung by ten hundred bees.

The soldiers left the wood and forest in shame,
But one was left behind because he was lame,
The animals felt sorry and took care of him,
Longer was he lame but now drenched in fame.

Antonia Gamage (9)
St Michael's CE VA Primary School, Lyme Regis

Sweet Unicorn

This unicorn was fun
And we played every day in the sun
She has a lovely horn
And we raced with a fawn.

She has a foal
Who looked in a hole
I like her warm touch
And I love her so much.

It's getting late
So I close the gate
She walked down the street
As I went to sleep.

Eleanor Shoesmith (10)
St Michael's CE VA Primary School, Lyme Regis

My Fish

One day at school I sat there so,
Working hard all day,
As I went home there was a big blow,
And there my fish did lay.

Dead she lay on the ledge of the pond,
Sad I lay on the floor,
Now I wish I had a magic wand,
I am so sad you must be sore.

I said to Mum, 'How can this be?'
Mum said, 'I do not know,'
Why did it have to happen to me,
All I did was sit down low.

The water had gone down,
That is how she died,
I am glad my other fish are safe and sound,
Next thing I did was just sighed.

Maybe my fish wanted to join the fish in the sea,
I wonder what she wanted to do,
I wonder if she wanted to have something different for tea,
I wish I could join her too.

So what do I do?
I might get another fish,
So I can play with it too,
For tea I will make it a big dish.

Robyn Lewis (9)
St Michael's CE VA Primary School, Lyme Regis

Majorettes

I love majorettes it's really fun,
I shall do it till I'm old,
I like to practise in the sun,
I'm so good so I'm told.

I won a cup to my delight,
It was really shiny,
It shined in the light,
It wasn't very tiny.

I held my cup and I was proud,
I couldn't believe my ears,
Look at all those people in the crowd,
I am almost in tears.

I passed my three year medal, that night,
The certificate was my reward,
My granny saw to my delight,
I definitely wasn't bored.

Granny called me over,
She was crying, she was so glad,
I felt I was in clover,
I thought I was going mad.

I went to get into the car,
I still couldn't believe it,
I felt like a movie star,
I wasn't sad not a bit.

Lillie Filtness (10)
St Michael's CE VA Primary School, Lyme Regis

My Life

When I was a little boy about three,
I got lost on the beach,
And stuck to me was a leach,
And they could not find me.

I played football at six,
I played sweeper,
And stopped at ten,
And played keeper.

Our team always won,
We had the best team,
When I went home I told my mum everything,
But she was very *mean!*

I like to eat chocolate,
I like to drink Coke,
I like to play football,
I am a bloke.

Next day I played cricket,
I bowled a ball they whacked it,
I bowled again I hit the wicket,
And then they were out.

I played till ten,
Stopped to play football,
We played against men,
We went to the mall.

Keiren White (10)
St Michael's CE VA Primary School, Lyme Regis

My Sister

My one and only sister,
Smily, cute and sweet,
I have news for my skin and blister,
She'll always be my treat.

She makes me happy,
And joyful too,
Her name is Ash,
Without her there is nothing to do.

She sometimes annoys me,
But I don't really care,
When she sits on my knee,
I play with her hair.

We go to the park,
But not when it's dark,
We play on the swings,
And all sorts of things.

Her long wavy hair,
A lovely golden brown,
Is so smooth and fair,
She always wears it down.

I do this and that,
She has funny ways,
I do that and this,
She is a great *sis*!

Charlie Taylor (9)
St Michael's CE VA Primary School, Lyme Regis

When I Tried To Run Away

One day I tried to run,
I tried to sprint,
Out the door to the leap,
But they all tried to stop me.

I had all my cash,
But I had to dash,
Out the door,
But they all tried to stop me.

I got pushed against the wall,
Until it almost broke,
Then I heard a call, I tried to see who it was,
But they all tried to stop me.

I'd heard my brother had run away,
He had gone to the park,
But how was I meant to get there,
I couldn't leave,
Cos they all tried to stop me.

I was not sad to go,
Why is it always me who tries to go,
Why is it always me who tries
To go, it's fun all alone, it's fun,
But they all tried to stop me.

Then I sat down on the sofa
My mum said she had done this when she was younger,
But I said you're a bit old for that
And then they didn't try to stop me.

Tom Wood (9)
St Michael's CE VA Primary School, Lyme Regis

My Grandad

One day my mum, she got a call
From my nan, she was unhappy.
She told my mum that grandad was ill,
He needed more than just a pill.

When I saw him, he was in pain,
I asked him, 'How are you?'
He said, 'I'm feeling fine,
But the pain keeps coming back all the time.'

When he is at home,
He gets a little angry,
When it hurts, he gets a cup of tea,
To calm the pain down.

My grandad had a sore wrist,
They put it in a white cast,
His arm was raised above his head,
I hope he would heal fast.

He came home the very next day,
I was surprised to see him,
I was that happy, I gave him,
A big hug, I never wanted to . . .
Let him go.

He goes to hospital every week,
To make sure it is healing fine,
I count his tablets every week,
So he can take them on time.

Billie-Mae Hoole (10)
St Michael's CE VA Primary School, Lyme Regis

My Special Fish

Every day I would go and look,
And give some food to eat,
My two friends were so much fun,
They were really quite neat.

I would look forward to seeing them,
Every single day,
They make me really happy,
They swim in a special way.

He got stuck in a pump,
And it really sucked him up,
Goldie got a huge big lump,
So we put him in a cup.

We went to the vet,
To ask him what was wrong,
He had to have surgery,
It was very, very long.

When we got him home,
We put Goldie into his container,
He was swimming along happily,
He looked a lot saner.

Poppy Kitcher (9)
St Michael's CE VA Primary School, Lyme Regis

A Lyme Limerick

My teacher at my school in Lyme,
Asked me to write him a rhyme,
He wanted a riddle that rhymed with Mr Kiddle,
But I could not come up with one on time.

Amy Hanlon (9)
St Michael's CE VA Primary School, Lyme Regis

I Lost My . . .

I lost my arm in the army,
I lost my leg in the navy.

I lost my socks in the butcher's shop
And I found them in my gravy.

I lost my teeth at the dentist,
I lost my arm in the army,
I lost my leg in the navy.

I lost my socks in the butcher's shop
And I found them in my gravy.

I lost my keys in the attic,
I lot my teeth at the dentist,
I lost my arm in the army,
I lost my leg in the navy.

I lost my socks in the butcher's shop
And I found them in my gravy.

Ryan Wood (9)
St Michael's CE VA Primary School, Lyme Regis

Crazy Teachers

Mr Kiddle winking
Mr Tozer soaking
Mrs Waterson thinking
Mrs Hammond choking.

Mrs Bayley crying
Mrs Kay baking
Mrs Blake flying
Mrs Deam faking.

Mrs Hyde sulking
Mrs Forder moaning
Mrs Dean's cat moulting
Mrs Gray phoning.

Rebecca Solway (9)
St Michael's CE VA Primary School, Lyme Regis

A True Poem About Rosie My Dog

She sat on her chair,
All on her own,
Wanting to get out,
So she chewed on her bone.

When we went to Thailand,
We had to give her away,
The people we gave her to had a child,
And they gave her away the next day.

After a year,
My grandad said,
'I have Rosie your dog,
Given to me by Fred.'

I'm so happy,
I could cry,
I was very sure,
She would never die.

On December the 13th,
She had a cold,
And went to sleep and died,
I was very quickly told.

I put my thoughts in my diary,
As I reflected on the past,
The memory of Rosie,
Will forever, ever last.

Phoebe Moksher Hill (9)
St Michael's CE VA Primary School, Lyme Regis

My Best Holiday

One day my friend said to me
Something very shocking.
'Can you come on holiday for free?'
I thought she was mocking.

I couldn't believe my ears,
What would my mum say?
I was almost in tears,
I couldn't wait to tell my mum the next day.

We went on a plane,
Turkey was the name.
It was better than a train,
And we played lots of games.

We had so much fun,
Playing in the pool,
All those days in the sun,
And just keeping cool.

We were on the way back,
I didn't want to go home,
But I did feel like a snack,
Inside I felt so alone.

I went for a week,
When I got back,
I went straight to sleep,
And that was that.

Katie Austin (10)
St Michael's CE VA Primary School, Lyme Regis

Best Friends

I have a best friend called Poppy,
But I've given her a nickname called Floppy,
I care for her, and she cares for me,
And I think she has a boyfriend called Lee.

I have a best friend called Lilly,
But sometimes she acts a bit silly,
She has a wonderful figure,
And a cat called Tigger.

I have a best friend called Aneesa,
But she hates eating pizzas,
She lives in a flat,
But does not have a cat.

I have a best friend called Rebecca Solway,
And her dad works at Colway,
She likes eating candy,
And I know she loves Andy.

I have a best friend called Abi,
But sometimes she thinks she's a bit flabby,
She can also ride a motorbike,
And she had a baby boy called Mike.

Tasmin Fowler (10)
St Michael's CE VA Primary School, Lyme Regis

My Baby Sister's Birth

When I was nine nearly ten,
At home with my mummy
She told me she was pregnant
She had a baby in her tummy.

I was struck with the news,
I didn't know how to feel
Should I be happy? Should I be sad?
The whole situation felt unreal.

I felt quite upset and sad,
Because I thought she was going
To take over the world,
But it wasn't that bad.

Now she is born,
All she ever does it eat,
She's got a lovely coat that is fawn,
And it looks really neat.

She is very sweet,
But always cries,
I like to give her a lovely treat,
I make her laugh and she gives a little sigh.

Now she is older,
She is much funnier,
But at night she gets colder,
I wish it would be sunnier.

Christina Street (10)
St Michael's CE VA Primary School, Lyme Regis

The First Time I Played For Lyme Under 7s

When I was 6 I played football,
I was the keeper as well as sweeper,
My first match,
I did a good catch,
But no one could get past me.

Dan was the best scorer,
We had a cheerleader called Laura,
I let in one goal,
There was a player called Cole,
But that was the only time they scored.

We won 9-1,
Then we all ate a bun,
I gave Keiran a nudge,
While he was eating a fudge,
And I'm glad I only let in one goal.

When we were home,
I brought a new cone,
When I got home I played my PlayStation,
I played my new game Elimination,
And I was unstoppable.

Jack was at my house,
I was the mouse,
Jack was the cat,
With a stinky mat.

I got mad,
And very sad,
My mum shouted at me,
To eat a kiwi,
But I hate kiwis.

I felt sick,
Jack took the mick,
We couldn't play,
So Jack had to go home.

Rhys Brown (10)
St Michael's CE VA Primary School, Lyme Regis

My Best Friend Billie-Mae

Once I met a friend
Her name was Billie-Mae
I give her stuff to lend
And we do everything the same.

My best friend Billie-Mae
When I need a friend, she's always there,
I play with her every day,
At school, at home, anywhere.

She is so kind, she is so nice,
We go to the beach
And in the winter we play on ice,
We share everything between us each.

We are good friends,
We always play,
She gives me stuff to lend,
We see each other every day.

Leah Wilkins (9)
St Michael's CE VA Primary School, Lyme Regis

Spring

Spring reminds me of
Daffodils and tulips, all colourful and bright,
Primroses and violets,
Like stars in the night.

Spring reminds me of
Butterflies, all gentle and light,
Little chicks,
Fluffy and white.

Spring reminds me of
Blossoms all over the trees,
People running away
Because of tiny little bees!

Landi Wagner (9)
St Thomas Garnet's School, Bournemouth

Snow

A clap of thunder
A bright lightning
Snow falling down
We wrapped up warm
Hats, boots and torches
Crunchy ice
With powdery snow
Made our fingers and noses glow.

Throwing freezing snowballs
As we giggled
Back inside
Nice and warm
With a hot chocolate
And memories of snow on the lawn.

Bryony Cook (10)
St Thomas Garnet's School, Bournemouth

Julian!

My name is Julian
I don't know why
I dislike it so much
I want to cry

I'd love it if my name was Jack
And 'Julian' I would never have back
So Jack it is then
Remember well
Tell all the world
By ringing a bell

So all the world
Will know just why
My name is Jack
And I won't cry!

Julian Osei-Bonsu (9)
St Thomas Garnet's School, Bournemouth

George

George is such a funny creature
With his feline grace and elegant features

With his four tiny paws
He can open doors

He's covered in fur
And he miaows then purrs

He would sleep all day
If he had his way

Then hunt all night
By the pale moonlight

His keen eyes see movement and he starts to chase
The next moment he's sitting and washing his face

He scratches and bites
And likes play fights

But there's nothing he likes better than a rub on the tummy
I really believe he thinks I'm his mummy.

Rebecca Murphy (10)
St Thomas Garnet's School, Bournemouth

My Friend From Mars

An alien took me to Mars
Where, guess what?
They drive around in cars.

They spend all day sitting in bars,
Laughing and drinking
And smoking cigars.

I think I'd like to live on Mars.

Philipp Antonas (9)
St Thomas Garnet's School, Bournemouth

Sounds

The rain pattering on the windowpane
The *roar!* of a plane just landing in Spain.
The cheer of a football crowd as a goal is scored.
The huff of me when I'm so bored.
The screech of a racing car.
The crack of a rifle from afar.
The scouts all round a campfire,
Or the noise of some children playing on a tyre.
The snort of a pig in a pigsty
And the bleat of a lamb very close by.
The noise of a jazzy saxophone,
Or a small dog chewing on a bone.
A congregation of people in a church hall,
While outside, children are playing with a ball.
The annoyance of a dripping tap,
Or the silent flutter of a flying bat.

Robert Degan (10)
St Thomas Garnet's School, Bournemouth

Hair

Long hair, short hair
Who really cares?
Spiky, red and straight
Black, green, what a state!

Curly, thick, up or down
Go to the hairdressers, don't hang around
Mousses, sprays, lots of gel
Not too much or Mother will yell

All I want is to be like Beckham
What do you reckon?

Broughton Sedgwick (9)
St Thomas Garnet's School, Bournemouth

Pets

Some pets are furry
Some pets are fun
Pets are made for everyone
You and me

Pets can be big, pets can be small
Pets can be thin, pets can be tall
Cats are playful, dogs are loud
Rabbits have fluffy tails like a cloud

I wonder if they understand us?
I talk to my pets every day
I don't know and you don't know
Pets don't know how to say.

Maria Degan (8)
St Thomas Garnet's School, Bournemouth

My Cat

My cat's name is Flossie
She's nearly five years old
She's mainly black with white boots on
Her eyes are green and bold.

She's always in the garden
And sometimes up a tree
She hunts around for birds and frogs
And brings them home for me.

She likes to sleep in flowerpots
She likes to sleep on the bed
And when the sun is shining bright
She sleeps on top of the shed.

She likes it when you stroke her
Especially whilst having a nap
But *suddenly* she'll scratch you
And that, I'm afraid, is that.

Katie Spencer (8)
St Thomas Garnet's School, Bournemouth

The Pet Shop

When I walked into the pet shop, what did I see?
Cute kittens and playful puppies all looking at me.
Slithering snakes, hungry hamsters and greedy guinea pigs too.
Can we find a pet for me and you?
Also, bouncing bunnies, beautiful birds and miniature mice.
I'd like them all . . . that would be nice!

Amy Mack-Nava (7)
St Thomas Garnet's School, Bournemouth

Sad

When I'm feeling sad
Because I've done something bad,
The thing I like the most
Is chocolate spread on toast.
Chocolate is best I'm sure,
When I'm eating it, I always want more!

Alice Winduss (7)
St Thomas Garnet's School, Bournemouth

The Cat

Once a cat went
To bed and woke up
One day late
He went
In the garden
And played
Catch the mouse
And he did!

Alexi Bullen (8)
St Thomas Garnet's School, Bournemouth

My Night

I flew to the sky and back too.
In the sky it was so bright blue.
The clouds were so white,
I thought it wasn't quite right
As it was night.
It gave me quite a fright.
But it was all right
Because my flight was just right
To be home by daylight.

Lewis Hawkins (7)
St Thomas Garnet's School, Bournemouth

Formula One

Cars speeding round the track,
I think one of the engines has a crack,
One of the drivers thinks his car's so flash,
Oh no, he's about to crash.

One of the drivers is on his last lap,
He can hear the spectators starting to clap,
He crosses the finish line for first place,
It is now the end of the big race.

Oliver Rickard (8)
St Thomas Garnet's School, Bournemouth

Rainforests

Rainforests are home to lots of creatures
And some of Mother Nature's special features
Spiders, lizards, birds that fly
Above the rainforest in the light blue sky
Hot, damp and humid too
And nettles that dig deep into your shoes
I think it's dangerous
You might think so too!

Kapil Chauhan (10)
St Thomas Garnet's School, Bournemouth

Birds

A wise old bird lived in an oak
The more he saw, the less he spoke
The less he spoke, the more he heard
I want to follow that wise old bird

Another wise bird lived in a cage
You would never see him in a rage
I hope I am like that when I reach his age

Another wise bird is rather slim
Everything about him looks quite trim
When I grow up, I would like to be like him

My last wise bird was free to fly
He made giant circles in the sky
I don't think I will be like him no matter how I try.

Delaney Dominey-Foy (8)
St Thomas Garnet's School, Bournemouth

Me And My Brother

Me and my brother,
we *do* really like each other.

He loves to paint but just look where it goes,
it's not just on the paper but also on his nose.

He loves to give his teddies a cuddle,
but just look at his room, it's such a muddle.

We are always told that the youngest goes to bed first,
but my brother always seems to have a thirst.

So off to bed we go together,
yes that is right, me and my brother.

Nadia Foy (7)
St Thomas Garnet's School, Bournemouth

The Cheetah

Faster than birds of the sky
Still slower than the speed of light
It lives in places that fry
It finds its home in branches tall
Never trust the cheetah, it always lies
And picks on creatures small
It looks like it can fly
They give people a fright
Why is it so deadly, why?
Is it small or is it big?
The sun may have a big sigh
For it is safe for a while
Since the beast has gone down for a lie
But after that it can run for a mile
Then chase the monsters high
Under his wonderful wing.

Tanja Wagner (11)
St Thomas Garnet's School, Bournemouth

The Rainforest

Welcome to my rainforest,
Where acid is dropping,
And the monkeys are mopping,
And where the trees come chopping down,
Where the birds fly,
And where the flowers grow,
And there the bees go.

But man is ruining our bounty,
This damage could destroy our land,
Quickly they chop the trees down,
They cause floods and dominate nature and land.

Jerome Paul (11)
St Thomas Garnet's School, Bournemouth

The Boar

I am a boar
My name is Bill
I live in the core
I pack a kick
It's got a big door
The bell makes a tick
My flatmate can soar
We've learnt not to kill
We've learnt it's rude to ignore
I must learn to sail
My boat must have the strength of a bull
I'm teaching him how to pour
And not to eat with his mouth full
He loves to snore
Soon we will make our trail.

Adam Whitney (10)
St Thomas Garnet's School, Bournemouth

The Rainforest

In the rainforest far away
The monkeys like to swing and play
Swinging high up in the trees
Sometimes they are hard to see,
Everyone looks up at them
Hiding in their leafy den.

There are lots of trees and birds,
Sometimes they are lost for words.
Snakes and tigers, people too,
The monkeys sometimes follow you!

Amy Spencer (10)
St Thomas Garnet's School, Bournemouth

The Lost Souls

I was assigned to the war,
So I had to fly without saying goodbye,
When I landed I was by the shore,
then I was put on a boat to sail,
Suddenly the sail tore,
So I had to bail,
The water came in more,
I thought I was going to die,
I started to roar,
There soon was a submarine on the same team,
It took me to shore,
I was taken to headquarters,
The people were poor,
They called my daughters,
They cooked me a boar,
And I met my wife, Katreen.

Declan Cosgrove (10)
St Thomas Garnet's School, Bournemouth

Rich

Neelam's house is so cool,
It even has a swimming pool.
She has Sky Plus,
Says it's a must,
But I just kept my cool.

Her dad's a paediatrician,
Her mum's an optician.
She's really rich,
But she's been ditched,
Finding a friend for her is a mission.

Natasha Coleman (11)
St Thomas Garnet's School, Bournemouth

The Rainforest

I used to live in the rainforest you know,
But it never really, really ever snows.
Some animals are rather cute,
But none of them wear a suit.
Most of them have long feet,
And they just look so very sweet.
Parrots, crocs and all the creatures
Have such very lovely features.
But now I wonder and I think
That they would lead me to the brink!
It rains so much you could fill a lake,
And the acid rain is not fake.
The food there is all rough and tough,
The animals realised it's not enough!
But then I looked up and saw,
I wasn't in the rainforest anymore.

Hannah Pickup (11)
St Thomas Garnet's School, Bournemouth

Stars

The stars seem to come out at night,
They shine and they're very bright,

Stars make the sky look very lit,
It's so nice to look at it,

When I go to bed I look at them,
They look like different coloured gems,

Stars form into unusual shapes,
They look like they seem to drape,

Shooting stars look like they're falling,
The noise of the night is people calling!

Kristy O'Donnell (11)
St Thomas Garnet's School, Bournemouth

Garden Life

I like the birds and the buzzing bees,
Better than the autumn trees.
All different kinds of flowers in spring,
The bluebirds as they sweetly sing.
The blazing yellow sun is shiny.
Some of the insects are so tiny.
The woodpeckers peck,
On their wooden deck.
The garden life is as live as can be,
And you don't even have to pay a fee.

Jana Browne (11)
St Thomas Garnet's School, Bournemouth

Music

Music, music
In my ears
You take away
All my fears

Music, music
You are fun
You cheer up
Everyone

Music, music
Always stay
Forever singing
Night and day.

Amber Cook (8)
St Thomas Garnet's School, Bournemouth

Winter

It was a wonderful sight,
For your eyes to see,
For the town was covered in a blanket of white.
Every cave was covered in icicles, every tree, in snow.
It was a wonderful sight
As you surely know.
To the children's delight,
They were allowed to play,
They didn't even have to put up a fight!
Every child wrapped up warm
So they didn't get a fright,
From the snow so cold.
They started a snowball fight,
Carrying as much snow as their gloved hands would hold,
Soon they decided to stop the fight,
But they had played from dusk 'til dawn.

Maeve Dunne (10)
St Thomas Garnet's School, Bournemouth

My Treasure

One day I went to find some treasure,
It filled me with lots of pleasure,
The treasure chest was filled with gold,
I knew it would buy me things 'til I'm old.
There were rubies, emeralds and money,
It made me think of sweet, sweet honey.
I felt so pleased when I found it,
I had definitely scored a hit!
I spent it with my own best friend,
Until it finally came to an end.

Hannah Elcock (11)
St Thomas Garnet's School, Bournemouth

Summer Breeze

Summer breeze, so softly blowing
In my garden, pinks are growing.
If you'll go and send the showers,
You may come and smell my flowers.

Jessica Smith (9)
St Thomas Garnet's School, Bournemouth

The Dolphin

The dolphin leaps
And with a splash,
Lands in the sea
And makes the waves crash.

The dolphin is so beautiful,
And so very sleek,
He is really, really fast,
With his long, pointed beak.

Because the dolphin is so powerful,
He is extremely fast,
Because he is extremely fast,
He is never, never last.

A shoal of dolphins,
Sleek and grey,
This is the way
They like to play.

Here are the dolphins,
So active and playful,
Man's best friend,
Can sometimes be helpful.

Alex Hoskins (10)
Salway Ash CE Primary School

The Pirate

The rocks struck the ship, stealing her skin,
Ripping a hole to let destiny in,
The last of the hell was for the mast to drop dead,
And the beckoning rocks a-listening,
Listening, whistling,
And the beckoning rocks a-listening,
As the ship submerged her head.

Some shouts were echoed from down below,
Down at the seabed where the waters flow,
Yet even hope had abandoned their days,
They're nothing but pirates,
Pirates, pirates,
They're nothing but pirates,
Or so the locals say.

The cries soon stopped and life was gone,
Twenty pirates, or sailors, and now there are none.
Except for the soul who chose not to rest,
The young captain's daughter,
His daughter, poor daughter,
Except for his daughter,
Who floated further west.

She clambered ashore on uncivilised land,
Where the palm trees were dying and there's dead yellow sand,
And a monkey clung to a swinging tree,
As it laughed hoarsely, and hoarsely choked,
And wheezily chuckled and wheezily spoke,
And it looked nervously at the new arrival to see.

A navy ship arrived that very following day,
To find a place where the daughter's body lay,
Her to lay forever (or at least for today),
Until the tide comes in and takes her,
Until the tide comes in and steals her,
But too soon the navy noticed the mark on her arm and went away,
'She's nothing but a pirate, or so the locals say.'

Finn Buchanan-Brown (10)
Salway Ash CE Primary School

The Maids

The sound of waves against a rock,
A voice of crystal, a flash of streaming hair,
A catch of laughter and then a glimmer of scales,
Then suddenly a crash, a bang, a thud of wood against rock,
More laughter, then a splash as something or someone
Plunged into the icy depths.

A bird of might swooped down upon the helpless crew,
Then off it flew towards its hungry chicks,
The distressed crew, they tried to swim,
But were clawed back by strong scaly hands,
They were the maids of the oceans,
But this was not known by the sailors,
And then the last sailor stopped his struggling,
And there were no signs suggesting what had happened.

Gabby Duff (10)
Salway Ash CE Primary School

Comforting Pets

Pets are friends that you may keep,
Round the house some might creep.
Dogs and cats through the day
Always want to come and play.
Budgies, parrots, screech and squawk,
Guinea pigs like to talk.
Protect a hamster in the house,
Gerbils or a tiny mouse.
Ponies, horses in the field,
Rabbits, canaries waiting for their meal.
Look after the donkey in the meadow,
You may name it buttercup yellow.
Keep a pet for a friend,
You'll find they're loyal in the end.

Katie Bakewell (10)
Thornford CE (VA) Primary School

Speedy Smart Cars

Cars, cars big and small
Everyone wants to have a car
It's just so cool
It will take you far, ever so far.

How many wheels, how many seats, it's up to you
The speed of the car goes much faster
Built to impress and that's what it's going to do
It is just the good old master.

Renault Clio it's got the spice
You just have to go, don't think twice
Yellow, green, red, or black
The colour I choose means I won't look back.

Ferrari Spider, Alfa Romeo,
Neither as good as a Lamborghini Morsalago
BMW it's got the speed
In a race it would lead.

Rob Helyar (11)
Thornford CE (VA) Primary School

Fruit

Fruit, fruit is good for my tummy
It is yummy and scrummy,
Big and small
But it does not matter to me
Because I like them all.
Orange and apple and banana too,
I eat them in the day
But not at night,
I eat them in a very big bunch,
I eat them quickly with a crunch.

Peter Miller (10)
Thornford CE (VA) Primary School

Acrobatic, Aquatic Friends

Dolphins here, dolphins there
Dolphins diving everywhere
Shimmering all night long
Making their clicking noise, click, click, click
Getting ready for another trick

Dolphins soaring through the sky
turning in the air
Whirling out from everywhere
Diving through the hoop
With his fellow troupe.

Chloe Beard (11)
Thornford CE (VA) Primary School

I Love Fruit

I love fruit,
Red, orange, green,
Delicious and juicy,
Better than a broad bean.

I love fruit,
Yellow and purple,
Red and green,
Murple, gurple, slurple.

I love peaches,
Lovely, delicious, with a munch,
Red, yellow and orange,
Crunch, munch and brunch.

Sam Jones (10)
Thornford CE (VA) Primary School

In The Rainforest

What do I see
Staring back at me?
It's a snake I see, like a piece of slithery rope
And it's staring under me.

What do I see
Staring at me?
It's a Koala I see, like a cuddly bear
And it's staring under me.

What do I see
Staring back at me?
It's a parrot I see, like a singing clown
And it's looking at me.

What do I see
Staring straight at me?
It's a tiger I see, like a pair of stripy pyjamas
And it's going to eat me!

Lauren Peters (10)
Thornford CE (VA) Primary School

Countryside

Animals playing in the wood
The corn swishing side to side
The grass is pointed
The worms slithering through the ground
Fox in the distance
Pheasant that you can just see
Rabbits in the fields
The breeze in the air
Look after the countryside
Please take care.

Jamie Appleby (9)
Thornford CE (VA) Primary School

Polar Bears

Playful polar bears rolling around,
In a cosy cave they can be found.
Cute cubs like to play fight,
All of their fur is a beautiful white.
Two thick layers of warm, snuggly fur,
When they're swimming, they're all a blur.
Fish will come like bees that swarm,
A velvet coat will keep them warm.

White, furry paws,
With sharp, pointed claws.
Their nose is black as coal.
In the snow they do roll.
Polar bears never get cold,
They are brave and they are bold.
There's lots more fun to be had,
Happy-go-lucky is the life they have.

Megan Taylor (11)
Thornford CE (VA) Primary School

Penguins

Oily and streamlined hunting their prey
Twishing and gliding through the waves
From Humboldt to Emperor
Big to small
They're all huddled together
Snug in a tight ball

Slipping and sliding, waddling too
With their big dinner jackets looking so new
As black as the night
As white as a cloud
Their bright yellow beaks look so proud.

Ellie Horsfield (10)
Thornford CE (VA) Primary School

The Countryside

The countryside - some trees that are alive
Some have a farm, and cows are calm
I'm happy there

The countryside - some trees that are alive
I see a river, bushes that quiver
I'm happy to be there

The countryside - some animals have died
it's such a shame, dead in the lane
Very sad to see

The countryside - it's great to be there
Lots of grass, as you pass
I like every bit of it

The countryside - I like the ride
A lot of ditches, fences and hedges
All around me at the edges

The countryside - the birds cried
You see a new flower, every single hour
I like every bit of it

The countryside - now the grass has dried
Some trees can be tall, some can be small
All better than a concrete wall!
I like every bit of it

The wonderful countryside - I like my ride
Get ready to cut the crops, the corn is the top
I like every bit of it.

Jonathon Legg (9)
Thornford CE (VA) Primary School

Who Am I?

Hills of sand
Make the land
Where I dwell
My owners sell
Who am I?

I have big, round eyes
That watch the skies
And big smelly feet,
You can't hear them beat
Who am I?

Long eyelashes have I
That make me cry,
A swishy tail that will not fail
Who am I?

Two fine humps,
They are not lumps!
I am used as a train
But not as a plane
Who am I?

Our land has drought,
But I'm like a spout,
No word of a lie
Or I'll spit in your eye!
Who am I?

Isobel Carretta (9)
Thornford CE (VA) Primary School

The Zoo

When we go to the zoo,
What do we see?
Fluffy yellow mane,
Huge balloon,
A long and short,
Smart suits
And a stripy pair of pyjamas,
There's long necks
And snappy teeth
All at one zoo.

When we go to the zoo
What do we see?
There's lazy lion
And slithering snakes,
Huge hippo and playful penguins,
Groovy giraffe
With a zooming zebra,
Everyone stays away from cruel croc.
What a lot of animals,
Such a funny lot!

Rachel Akerman (10)
Thornford CE (VA) Primary School

Holiday Poem

Holiday, holiday
Is so much fun
I can't wait to lie in the sun
Dive in the pool
Nice and cool.

Tezra Sculthorpe (9)
Thornford CE (VA) Primary School

The Tree

It was like a spider
Which rested in a park
Happy and quiet
Swaying very slowly

It was some pink candyfloss
In the colourful spring
It had vast blossoms
And it swished gently

It was as big as a monster
In the sunny summer
It had green leaves
And it moved peacefully

It was like a bald patch on your head
In the freezing winter
All cold and bare
And it whistled quietly

It was a green cloud
Which never wanted to leave
But one day the tree was . . . *gone!*

Vivienne Greening (10)
Thornford CE (VA) Primary School

Stop The Pollution

I'm travelling to the city
I found it very loud
sirens screaming suddenly
I couldn't stand the crowd
The pollution was so bad
Murky black, foggy smoke
Believe me, it's not a joke.

Aaron FitzGerald (10)
Thornford CE (VA) Primary School

My Own Little World

Forever, a snow-white cloud, will carry me away,
But wait! My vision is starting to fade away,
Then I open my eyes to the start of another day,
Another day, another day, I have to go to school today,
I look at the horses, they start to neigh,
On the farm, it's a boring day,
But tonight my dreams will come,
But then they'll fade away.

Green sand, mile-long snake,
Blue trees, purple lake,
Round houses underground,
When the birds sing that lovely sound.

Infinite ice cream,
Chocolate cone,
Dragons make
Brand new home.

In human life, murder and theft,
Cars crashed and children hurled,
But that will never happen in my dreams,
Because I'm the creator of my own little world.

Paul Manton (10)
Thornford CE (VA) Primary School

Horses

Trotting round fields of green grass
Rabbits running as I see them pass
I feel the wind through my flowing mane
I'm running in the rain down the lane

Galloping when I race
At a very fast pace
Listening to people cheer
The finishing post is so very near.

Charlotte Mouncey (9)
Thornford CE (VA) Primary School

In The Jungle

Mippo the hippo
Ate a giant-sized Calippo
On a Sunday morning
But when it came to Monday
He found it very boring.

Jake the snake
Baked a very large cake
On a Tuesday morning,
But when it came to Wednesday
He lay in bed all day.

Larrot the parrot
Ate a huge carrot
On a Thursday morning,
But when it came to Friday
You should see how he was soaring.

Miranda the panda
Was eating a banana
On a Saturday morning,
But when it came to Sunday
She sat on the veranda.

Hayley Peters (10)
Thornford CE (VA) Primary School

Winter

It's snowed outside, so my sister said,
'I'll stay inside and huggle my ted.'
She saw me playing in the snow
So she got out of bed and out she goes.

The slippery sledge
Goes into the hedge,
A snowball fight
Gives her a fright.
A snowman is much taller than her.
She said her favourite season's winter.

Nathan Thompson (9)
Thornford CE (VA) Primary School

Countryside

In the peaceful countryside
Where the tractor chugs
We are going for a walk
With a picnic rug

We see the hunters shooting
At the poor birds
Under the big
Tremendous herds
This is not the place for us

We went to the wood where we saw no wrong
So we set out the rug but smelt a horrible pong
This is not the place for us

We saw the lumberjacks
Cutting down the trees
Covered in swarms of
Stinging bees
A battle is raging amid the buzz

We left the countryside
In our car
Heading at speed towards the Spar
This is the place for us
But then we think, home is the place for us.

Jonathan Dolbear (10)
Thornford CE (VA) Primary School

Jungle

What's this I see? Two bright eyes looking at me.
Tiger, tiger, running bright through the forests of the night,
Orange sun . . . bright, what a brilliant sight!

What's this I see? Two bright eyes looking at me.
Monkey, monkey, swinging high, like a small brown ball,
Look as he goes swinging by,
Don't stand around and let him die.

What's this I see? Two bright eyes looking at me.
Crocodile, crocodile swimming by, like a log,
Trying to catch fish as he jumps up high,
Don't stand around and let him die.

What's this I see? Two bright eyes looking at me.
Parrot, parrot flying by, looking like a colourful cloud,
Flapping up very high,
Don't stand around and let him die.

What's this I see? Two bright eyes looking at me.
Snake, snake, wiggling by, like a rope,
He can't cope,
If you trade his trees for a bar of soap.

Tree, tree standing tall, they chop him down,
So people can play ball.
Use your head or they'll all be . . . dead.

Will Davies (9)
Thornford CE (VA) Primary School

On The Farm

I look in the pigsty, what do I see?
A huge pink snout looking at me.
I look in the house, what do I see?
people sitting down, eating their tea.
I look in the shed, what do I hear?
Two fat rats squeaking in fear.
I look in the barn, what do I hear?
A little purring cat somewhere near.
I look in the garage, what do I find?
Four newborn kittens all fluffy and blind.
I look in the porch, what do I find?
A little black puppy that whined and whined.

Charlotte Gordge (10)
Thornford CE (VA) Primary School

School

Everybody likes to learn,
Teachers help by teaching,
Children help by listening.
Teachers play games with children,
Children like to learn.
Teachers inform pupils,
Students listen to the trainer.
Teachers like to educate,
Informers instruct maths and English.
Children don't like it,
So teachers like to educate.

Alex Thorne (9)
Thornford CE (VA) Primary School